INCLUSION AND SCHOOL IMPROVEMENT

INCLUSION AND SCHOOL IMPROVEMENT

A PRACTICAL GUIDE

RITA CHEMINAIS

David Fulton Publishers

London

David Fulton Publishers Ltd
The Chiswick Centre, 414 Chiswick High Road, London W4 5TF

www.fultonpublishers.co.uk

First published in Great Britain by David Fulton Publishers 2002

Note: The right of Rita Cheminais to be identified as the author of this work has been asserted by her in accordance with the Copyright, Designs and Patents Act 1988.

British Library Cataloguing in Publication Data
A catalogue record for this book is available from the British Library.

ISBN 1-84312-005-4

Typeset by Keyset Composition, Colchester
Printed in the United Kingdom by Hobbs the Printers Ltd

Contents

Acknowledgements

My interest in inclusive education at a strategic level arose from my involvement in delivering the OFSTED school self-evaluation course in Tameside LEA, during 2001–2.

In preparing this second book on inclusion and school improvement, I sought the views of senior managers, Special Educational Needs Coordinators (SENCOs) and Inclusion Coordinators working in Tameside schools and services. I am appreciative of the support systems they identified as being crucial to sustaining educational inclusion in schools.

I am also deeply indebted to my colleagues in the Special Educational Needs Service Unit and the Educational Psychology Team, who have continued to enlighten me in relation to making inclusion happen in schools, while supporting a framework of best value principles.

I am grateful to Ian Smith, Chief Education Officer; Margaret Ralph-Hawthorne, Head of School Improvement in Tameside; and also to Ian Chambers, Leader of the Continuing Professional Development Team within the Tameside Monitoring and Advisory Team, for giving me the opportunity to disseminate my knowledge and expertise on inclusion to an audience of interested and committed educational professionals and practitioners within Tameside schools, and also in other neighbouring LEAs.

My thanks go to Pauline Collier, SEN Adviser in Bury LEA, for her support and encouragement in enabling me to produce this follow-up to my earlier publication entitled *Developing Inclusive School Practice*.

I am grateful to colleagues at the Centre for Special Education, University College Worcester, especially Joe Hodgson, and to Jenny Goodwin, at Manchester Metropolitan University, for their continuing interest, support, valued experience, constructive comments and informed feedback about my publications.

I wish to thank my family and friends for their patience and endurance in supporting me during the writing of this book. They continue to tolerate my nocturnal writing activities, and maintain my sanity.

While every effort has been made to acknowledge sources throughout the book, such is the range of inclusion aspects covered, however, that I may have unintentionally omitted to mention their origin. If so, I offer my apologies to all concerned.

Abbreviations

AEN	additional educational needs
AOB	any other business
AST	advanced skills teacher
CAD	computer-aided design
CAL	computer-assisted learning
CD-ROM	compact disc – read only memory
COP	Code of Practice
CPD	continuing professional development
CSIE	Centre for Studies on Inclusive Education
DfEE	Department for Education and Employment
DfES	Department for Education and Skills
DVD	digital video discs
EAL	English as an additional language
EBD	emotional and behavioural difficulties
EBSD	emotional, behavioural and social difficulties
EDP	Education Development Plan
EFQM	European Foundation for Quality Management
HMI	Her Majesty's Inspector
IAT	Inclusion Advisory Team
ICT	information and communications technology
IEP	Individual Education Plan
ILRC	inclusive learning resource centre
INSET	in-service education and training
KS	key stage
LEA	Local Education Authority
LSA	Learning Support Assistant
NASEN	National Association for Special Educational Needs
NLNS	National Literacy and Numeracy Strategies
NQT	newly qualified teacher
OASIS	Open Access Supporting Inclusive Study
OFSTED	Office for Standards in Education
PANDA	Performance and Assessment Report
PICSI	Pre-Inspection Context and School Indicator Report
PSHE	personal, social and health education
PSP	pastoral support programme

SEN   special educational needs
SENCO   Special Educational Needs Coordinator
SIP   School Improvement Plan
SMT   senior management team
SSE   school self-evaluation
SWOT   strengths, weaknesses, opportunities and threats
TA   Teaching Assistant
TSB   Trustee Savings Bank
TTA   Teacher Training Agency

Introduction

Inclusion and school improvement

Inclusive education is concerned with responding to individual needs in a problem-solving way. In order to enable schools to fully support educational inclusion, teachers in particular need to be given the time, outside the classroom, to plan and prepare for meeting a diversity of pupils' learning needs more effectively.

Teachers remain the key to raising standards. It is vital that they understand the principles of curriculum differentiation, and apply these consistently within their own classroom context, in order to reduce the barriers to learning and participation, and to support inclusive learning, through high quality teaching. In practice this means that all teachers will:

- show respect for pupils' individual learning styles and differences;
- be responsive to pupils' different learning styles;
- use different levels of tasks and activities;
- utilise a range of teaching strategies;
- teach thinking skills consistently across the curriculum.

An inclusive school is a listening institution, whereby the views and opinions of all stakeholders – senior managers, teaching and non-teaching staff, pupils, parents, governing body and community partners – are valued. An inclusive school is receptive to change, and provides value for money.

Inclusive education is synonymous with high quality teaching and learning. The effectiveness of inclusive education will be evident in the improvement in the quality of teaching and learning across the curriculum, in order to meet a diversity of learners' needs.

Inclusive schools involve parents and pupils as consumers. They value and celebrate individuals' achievements. It is vital that schools become more open in their approach to inclusive education by ensuring that pupils are able to express their views on the success or otherwise of particular teaching and learning strategies that they have experienced, in order to inform and improve inclusive practice. This more open and reflective approach requires schools to utilise a system of school self-evaluation that supports inclusive education for all pupils.

Inclusion paves the way for school improvement and effectiveness. In schools where all pupils are included and where the teaching and learning have been developed to meet specific needs, achievement for all pupils has been seen to improve faster than in schools with a non-inclusive ethos.

(Disability Equality in Education 1999)

The Inclusion Coordinator continues to be a driving force in moving inclusion forward within the educational setting. The SEN Co-ordinator (SENCO) is often best placed to become the Inclusion Coordinator, in view of their experience and skills in focusing on the appropriate strategies to enable a diversity of children to gain curriculum access.

Indicator B.2.3 (ii) of the Index for Inclusion asks the question:

Does the school call its co-ordinator of support a learning support or inclusion co-ordinator, rather than a 'special educational needs co-ordinator'?

(Booth and Ainscow 2000: 70)

What is the aim of this book?

The aim of this book is to enable all those involved in inclusive education to understand:

- their roles and responsibilities in supporting inclusive culture, policy and provision;
- how to identify and remove barriers to learning and participation in inclusive educational settings;
- the importance of utilising a model of school self-evaluation to raise standards in inclusive education;
- the importance of continuing professional development for all staff, on improving the quality of teaching and learning to meet a diversity of pupils' individual learning needs.

Who is this book for?

- Head teachers and senior managers in school and further education colleges;
- SENCOs, Learning Support Managers, Inclusion Coordinators working in a range of educational settings;
- Local Education Authority (LEA) advisers, inspectors, school improvement officers, strategic managers for inclusive education;
- educational psychologists;
- senior education lecturers in higher education;
- governors with responsibility for inclusion.

How is the format designed?

- To act as a point of quick reference to senior managers, Inclusion Coordinators and SENCOs.
- To support the continuing professional development of Inclusion Coordinators, SENCOs, and all those involved in supporting inclusive school culture, policy and practice.
- To enable pages to be photocopied for training purposes, within the purchasing institution.

Part 1

Professional development to support inclusion

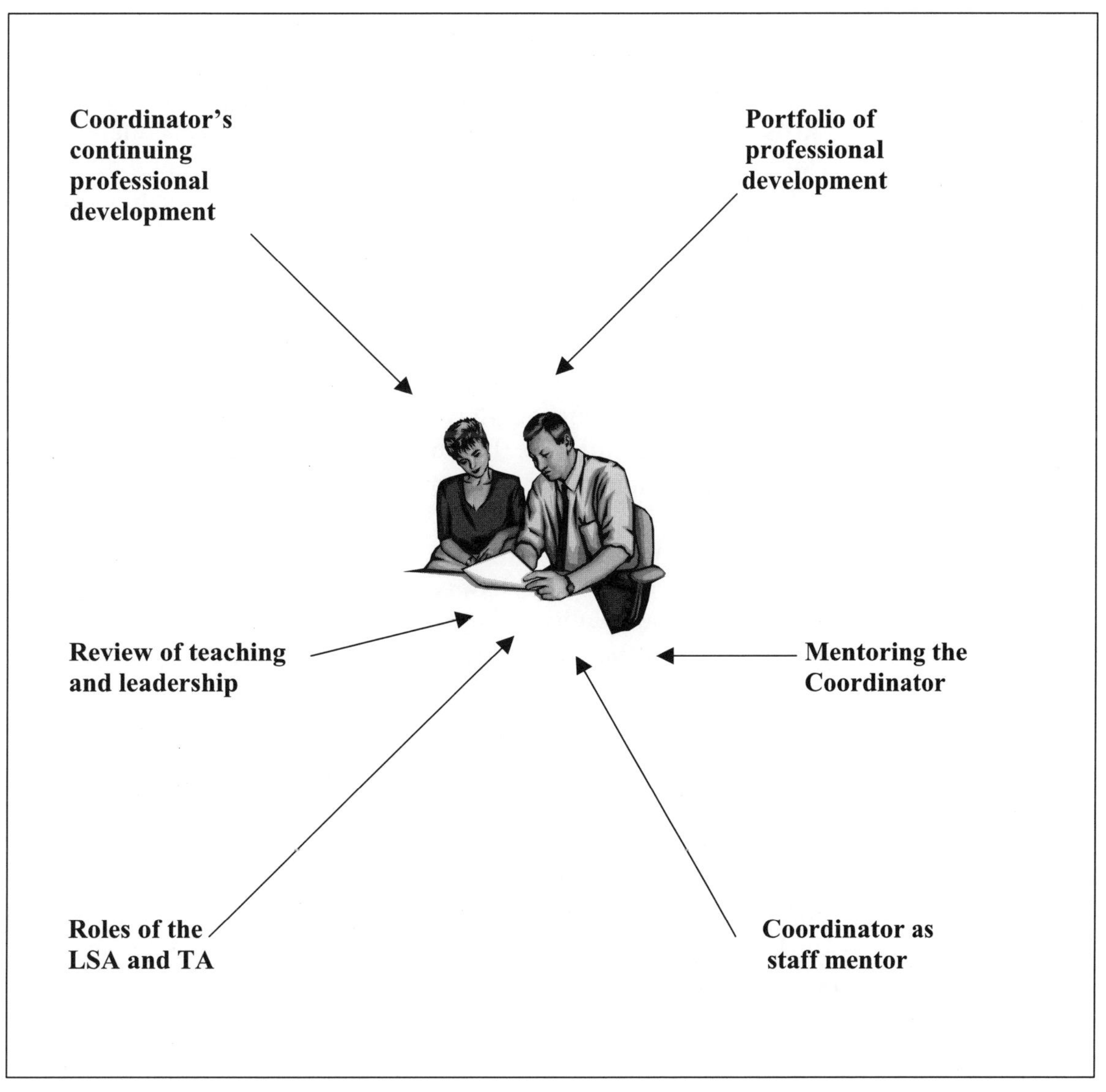

The Inclusion Coordinator would be well advised to compile an ongoing portfolio of professional development, linked to meeting the Teachers' Standards Framework (DfES 2001a). This record of evidence will support and reflect upon the progress made by the Inclusion Coordinator, in promoting and improving educational inclusion within the school.

The portfolio ideally would be divided into two sections:

Section 1: Evidence of achievements, e.g. certificates, qualifications, relevant courses attended, posts held and particular responsibilities.

Section 2: Records of the Inclusion Coordinator's experience, skills and attributes, e.g. evidence of team building, collaborative working, motivating others; analysis of strengths and areas for further development; priorities and future plans, further qualifications.

The Inclusion Coordinator is likely to wish to reflect on:

- values held as a manager and teacher;
- aspects of their role in which they excel;
- particular contributions they have made to the school;
- an important initiative they have led recently;
- aspects of their work that prevent them from achieving their objectives;
- the main challenge(s) in their role;
- the aspects of their present role that they wish to develop;
- the skills and qualities that they need to develop;
- the nature of the support that would enable them to make more of their role.

The Inclusion Coordinator's portfolio of professional development may be kept in a ring binder or stored electronically. It will form part of their self-review towards meeting performance objectives.

An example of what to include in a portfolio of professional development is outlined in the checklist on the following page.

The in-service education training (INSET) manager in any school would need to support the Inclusion Coordinator in working towards compiling a portfolio of professional development.

Checklist for a portfolio of professional development

- ☐ Job description matched to the Teachers' Standards Framework
- ☐ Outcomes from a professional development audit
- ☐ Curriculum vitae listing qualifications, specialist skills, work-related achievements, membership of working parties/committees and professional organisations, publications, action research
- ☐ Professional development action plan with threshold assessment evidence
- ☐ Annual record of training attended and delivered, with evidence of dissemination impact
- ☐ Summaries of leading articles read related to educational inclusion and relevant materials from courses attended
- ☐ Evidence of monitoring school inclusion, e.g. lesson observations and feedback information, analysis of pupil performance data to indicate value added, outcomes from scrutiny of teachers' planning, IEPs and pupils' work, outcomes from discussions with pupils, teachers and support staff regarding pupil progress and inclusive provision
- ☐ Evidence of supporting the professional development of others, Learning Mentors, Learning Support Assistants (LSAs)
- ☐ Discussion papers prepared and produced for significant inclusion meetings
- ☐ Minutes of meetings with the inclusion team, senior management team (SMT), inclusion governor
- ☐ Self-evaluation evidence – reflections on personal effectiveness and impact
- ☐ Record of progress in meeting the Teachers' Standards Framework, e.g. mentoring evidence
- ☐ Evidence of significant communication and consultation with parents and pupils, which promotes best inclusive practice
- ☐ Evidence of using school self-evaluation audit tools, e.g. the Index for Inclusion, OFSTED framework for school self-evaluation or the EFQM Excellence Model to evaluate inclusive culture, policy and practice within the school
- ☐ Reports on the outcome of visits to other schools to observe best inclusive practice
- ☐ Examples of any bids put forward for additional funding for inclusion projects, extra-curricular involvement
- ☐ Evidence of inclusion budget management
- ☐ Multimedia evidence of contributions to enhancing school inclusive practice, e.g. CD-ROM, video production, photographs, school inclusion website, power point presentations
- ☐ A copy of any school policies involving the Inclusion Coordinator, e.g. teaching and learning policy, gifted and talented policy, inclusion policy
- ☐ A copy of the annual governing body report to parents on the effectiveness of the school's inclusion policy and provision
- ☐ A copy of the Inclusion Action Plan
- ☐ Summary reports showing involvement in summer schools or Excellence in Cities projects.

The role of the Inclusion Coordinator is wide-ranging and requires a regular review of the professional development requirements needed to meet the aspects within the ten dimensions of the DfES Teachers' Standards Framework (July 2001).

The model audit that follows, which is based on the DfES Framework for Teaching and Leadership, can be used as a mechanism for setting objectives in relation to the Inclusion Coordinator's performance management assessment process.

It would be useful for the Inclusion Coordinator to consider the following issues:

- whether they meet all the aspects in each dimension;
- whether there are some aspects that suit their skills in working with particular types of children, but that do not cover the full diversity of pupils, e.g. little previous experience of working with emotional and behavioural difficulties (EBD) or gifted and talented pupils;
- whether they are already competent in a particular dimension to such an extent that they are able to mentor, train and support other staff;
- whether they require further support and training in order to further develop their own abilities in a particular dimension.

The expectations for the Inclusion Coordinator under each of the ten dimensions of teaching and leadership are outlined in the Teaching and Leadership Audit that follows. This is based on the DfES Framework, and meets the OFSTED school inspection requirements in relation to judging the quality of leadership and management within educational settings.

Inclusion Coordinator's Audit for Teaching and Leadership

Indicate how confident you are about the aspects of each dimension by rating your skill confidence level on a scale of 1-3.

(1 = not confident; 2 = fairly confident; 3 = confident/competent).

1. Knowledge and understanding

- Characteristics of effective teaching and learning styles ___
- Main strategies for improving/sustaining high standards of pupil achievement ___
- Promoting pupils' spiritual, moral, social and cultural development and their good behaviour ___
- Applying the strategies to support pupils with additional educational needs (AEN) ___
- Use of information and communications technology (ICT) to improve pupils' curriculum access ___
- Use of ICT to aid teaching and learning ___
- Use of ICT as a means of communication between those teaching pupils with more complex AEN ___
- Application of relevant research, national inspection evidence and legislation to meet AEN pupils' needs ___
- Effective communication of information to LEAs, external agencies, parents, other schools and colleges on transfer ___
- Contributing to the professional development of other staff in relation to AEN and inclusion ___
- How to recognise and deal with stereotyping in relation to disability, race/ethnicity, gender, ability ___
- Leading the formulation, planning, implementation and review of Individual Education Plans (IEPs), individual pupil action plans, pastoral support programmes (PSPs) ___

2. Planning and setting expectations

- Analyse and interpret relevant national, local and school data, plus any research and inspection evidence to inform educational inclusion, expectations, targets and teaching methods ___
- Work with pupils, subject leaders, class teachers with pastoral/tutorial responsibilities and LSAs, and Learning Mentors to ensure that realistic expectations of behaviour and achievements are set for AEN pupils ___

3. Teaching and managing pupil learning

- Identify and disseminate the most effective teaching approaches for pupils with AEN ___
- Monitor the effectiveness of appropriate teaching and learning activities ___
- Set targets to meet pupils' AEN ___
- Support the development of improvements in literacy, numeracy and ICT and access to the wider curriculum ___
- Identify and develop study skills to support pupils in their ability to work independently and learn more effectively ___
- Lead and develop effective liaison between schools cross-key stage or phase to ensure continuity in terms of support and progression in pupils' learning ___

4. Assessment and evaluation

- Collect and interpret specialist assessment data on AEN pupils and use it
  to inform inclusive practice _____
- Devise, implement and evaluate systems for identifying, assessing and
  reviewing AEN pupils in relation to the school's inclusion policy _____
- Provide regular information to the head teacher and governing body on the
  evaluation of the effectiveness of inclusive provision for pupils with AEN,
  to inform decision making and policy review _____

5. Pupil achievement

- Support staff in understanding the learning needs of AEN pupils and the
  importance of raising their achievement _____
- Monitor the progress made in setting objectives and targets for AEN pupils _____
- Assist in the evaluation of and the effectiveness of teaching and learning and
  use the analysis to guide further improvement _____
- Ensure the establishment of opportunities for the Inclusion Coordinator,
  LSAs, Learning Mentors and other teachers to review the needs, progress
  and targets of pupils with AEN _____

6. Relations with parents and wider community

- Develop and maintain effective partnerships between parents and the school's
  staff so as to promote pupils' learning _____
- Communicate effectively with parents to provide information about their
  child's targets, achievements and progress _____
- Develop effective liaison with external agencies in order to provide maximum
  support for AEN pupils _____

7. Managing own performance and development

- Chair reviews, case conferences and meetings effectively _____
- Judge when to make decisions and when to consult with others, including
  external agencies _____
- Prioritise and manage own time effectively to balance the demands of
  administration, teaching and advisory work with colleagues _____
- Take responsibility for own professional development _____

8. Managing and developing staff and other adults

- Encourage all members of staff to recognise and fulfil their statutory
  responsibilities to pupils with AEN _____
- Advise, contribute to and coordinate the professional development of staff
  to increase their effectiveness in responding to pupils with AEN _____
- Provide support and training to trainees and newly qualified teachers (NQTs)
  in relation to understanding the needs of AEN pupils, and raising their
  achievement and attainment _____
- Support staff by ensuring that all involved have the necessary information to
  secure improvements in teaching and learning, and disseminate good
  practice in AEN across the school _____
- Support staff in developing pupils' understanding of the duties, opportunities,
  responsibilities and rights of citizens _____

9. Managing resources

- Establish staff and resource requirements to meet the needs of pupils with AEN   ___
- Advise the head teacher, SMT and governing body of likely priorities for expenditure and allocate resources available efficiently to meet the objectives of the inclusion policy, to maximise pupils' achievements and to ensure value for money   ___
- Deploy or advise the head teacher on the deployment of staff involved in working with AEN pupils to ensure most efficient use of teaching and other expertise   ___
- Organise and coordinate the deployment of learning resources, including ICT, and monitor their impact and effectiveness   ___
- Maintain existing resources and explore opportunities to develop or incorporate new resources from the wide range of sources inside and outside the school   ___

10. Strategic leadership

- Contribute effectively to the development of a positive inclusive ethos in which all pupils have access to a broad, balanced and relevant curriculum, which contributes to their spiritual, moral, cultural, mental and physical development, in preparing them for adult life experiences   ___
- Ensure the objectives of the inclusion policy are reflected in the school improvement plan   ___
- Ensure that effective systems are in place to identify and meet needs and that they are coordinated, monitored, evaluated and reviewed   ___
- Set standards and provide examples of best practice for other teachers in identifying, assessing and meeting pupils' AEN   ___

Mentoring the Coordinator

Although the Inclusion Coordinator is likely to be a member of the senior management team, they will benefit considerably from having a mentor (line manager) within the school. This mentor will provide positive support to the Coordinator, in order to enable them to fulfil the role expectations identified in the previous Teaching and Leadership Audit.

The mentor ideally should be a deputy head teacher, or perhaps the head teacher in a small school. Access periodically to an external expert, e.g. the school Link Adviser, Senior Adviser or the LEA Inclusion Consultant, can be valuable in supporting the Inclusion Coordinator's continuing professional development (CPD) in specific aspects of the role, where the school cannot provide the necessary experience.

Mentoring is a positive mechanism and activity for developing the management skills of the Inclusion Coordinator (as mentee) as well as those of the mentor.

The mentoring relationship will be based upon:

- a clearly understood, transparent procedure;
- an understanding of each other's role as mentor and mentee;
- a relationship of trust;
- the mentor having credibility within the school;
- confidentiality, discretion and sensitivity;
- the mentee recognising their own continuing professional development needs;
- the mentor having a repertoire of necessary skills, e.g. planner, organiser, negotiator, change agent, good listener, counsellor, analyser, reflective practitioner, critical friend;
- the mentor challenging the mentee in inverse proportion to success;
- the mentee taking the necessary action;
- sufficient quality time being made available in school for mentoring to take place.

The mentor will assist the Inclusion Coordinator in developing skills that will support future career aspirations. They will also help the Inclusion Coordinator to set personal and professional development objectives, and identify ways of implementing them, in order to meet the DfES Teachers' Standards Framework, in relation to teaching and leadership.

The Coordinator will need to decide their individual development priorities by considering:

- the national standards they need to improve in;
- the expectations and responsibilities assigned to their role;
- the role changes that require new skills, e.g. the use of ICT as a management tool;
- the findings from research evidence about what makes effective teachers, managers and leaders in school;
- their ability to manage, coach and develop other staff, i.e. NQTs, Learning Mentors, LSAs, Teaching Assistants (TAs);

- the amount and nature of support and professional development required to fulfil a particular role.

The Coordinator will gain maximum benefit from mentoring when:

- opportunities are provided to learn from and observe other colleagues and Inclusion Coordinators in other schools;
- the mentor and Inclusion Coordinator work together on resolving real school issues that will lead to developing improved inclusive practice;
- focus is given to targeting specific Inclusion Coordinator skill training, which can be applied back into whole-school classroom practice, and which improves barrier-free learning and participation opportunities for the full diversity of pupils;
- the Inclusion Coordinator has the opportunity to reflect upon their own practice;
- the Inclusion Coordinator has the confidence to try out new ideas and strategies;
- regular feedback on the Inclusion Coordinator's changing practice is provided by the mentor.

The outcome and impact of mentoring the Coordinator must result in an improvement in pupils' learning and achievements, as well as an increase in the percentage of good quality teaching delivered to a diversity of children throughout the school.

Illustrated on the next page is a suggested proforma for recording mentoring meetings with the Inclusion Coordinator. This evidence can be incorporated into their portfolio of professional development.

Record of mentoring meeting with the Inclusion Coordinator	
Participants:	**Date and time of meeting:**
Main focus of the meeting:	
Evidence of successful progress:	
Area(s) for further development:	
Focus for the next meeting:	
Date and time of next meeting:	
Signed: ___________________________ ___________________________	
(Mentor) (Inclusion Coordinator)	

10

The Inclusion Coordinator in their mentoring role should:

- be purposeful, inclusive and values-driven;
- embrace the inclusive and distinctive school context;
- promote an active view of learning;
- be instructionally focused;
- spread their good practice throughout the school;
- build capacity by developing the school as a learning community;
- be strategically driven and futures-oriented;
- be developed through innovative and experiential methods;
- be supported by a coherent and fully understood inclusion policy.

A crucial dimension of their mentoring role in creating an inclusive school community is to develop staff abilities to improve barrier-free learning opportunities for a diversity of pupils. This will largely be undertaken through clear communication and joint work with other teachers and support staff, in how to enhance access to the curriculum, for individual pupils with additional educational needs. The Inclusion Coordinator will play a crucial part in providing a staff development programme on improving inclusive practice, in consultation with the senior management team and other colleagues in the school.

The Coordinator as a mentor to staff helps to raise staff confidence, improve attitudes to inclusion and increase inclusion skills. They act as a positive role model, an adviser and an experienced critical but supportive friend to staff who require specific or additional help to improve their inclusive practice.

A framework for successful mentoring

- Establish the aims and objectives of the mentoring programme.
- Clarify the resources and time required to provide quality mentoring to staff.
- Indicate how success will be measured and recorded.
- Set targets with staff and clarify the focus for the mentoring programme.
- Make clear administrative procedures, e.g. period of notice required if mentoring meetings inadvertently have to be cancelled and rearranged; what the point of reference is if personal contact in school is unavailable, such as telephone support or email conferencing to provide supplementary information and answer queries.
- Provide feedback on progress to the mentee and ongoing support.
- Monitor progress of the Inclusion Coordinator as both mentor and mentee, by involving a third party, e.g. head teacher, deputy head teacher or external consultant/adviser.
- Evaluate the outcomes and impact of the mentoring programme provided, and use this to improve future support to other colleagues

The Learning Support Assistant, as a member of a collaborative teaching and learning team, is central to developing effective educational inclusion. In order that they contribute to best value and promote an inclusive ethos by sharing skills and supporting others, the LSA needs time to reflect upon and learn from their experience.

The role of the LSA is broader and more demanding in an inclusive school, catering for a diversity of pupils, for several reasons.

- The LSA will be working with a diversity of pupils with additional educational needs.
- A higher level of ICT and multimedia expertise will be required.
- The LSA will need to be more flexible, independent, self-managing and reliant on using their initiative in creative ways.
- Secure knowledge about curriculum differentiation, teaching and learning styles and P/NC attainment level descriptors will be a necessity, in order to participate fully in delivering INSET and providing support to teachers, other support staff, pupils and parents, with confidence.
- The LSA is expected to achieve more immediate successful inclusive learning outcomes within shorter time limits.
- They will be committed to working longer hours, beyond the school day, and in return, will be suitably recompensed.
- They will require ongoing mentoring from the Inclusion Coordinator, particularly in relation to managing potential conflict among their client group.
- The LSA should have a more permanent employment contract which is not reliant on fluctuating temporary funding.

The LSA should receive an appropriate programme of induction and support. They will require access to ongoing opportunities for continuing professional development and career development.

Learning
Support
Assistant
job
description

Index for Inclusion Indicator C.1.10

1. Are LSAs involved in curriculum planning and review?
2. Are LSAs attached to a curriculum area?
3. Are LSAs concerned to increase the participation of all pupils?
4. Do LSAs maximise pupil independence from their direct support?
5. Do LSAs encourage peer support of pupils who experience barriers to learning?
6. Do LSAs avoid hampering pupils' relationships with their peers?
7. Are LSAs' views sought about the nature of their job description?

(Booth and Ainscow 2000: 86)

Outlined on the following page is an example of a job description for an LSA. This is only a suggested model, which is designed to operate within the context of a whole-school barrier-free teaching and learning culture and ethos.

Learning Support Assistant

JOB DESCRIPTION

Responsible to: the Inclusion Coordinator (line manager).

Responsible for: promoting and securing barrier-free teaching and learning opportunities for a diversity of pupils with additional educational needs (AEN).

Principal purpose: to support a whole-school response to educational inclusion; to provide guidance and support to staff on inclusive classroom practice; to work in partnership and liaise closely with the Inclusion teacher and the Inclusion Coordinator.

Main duties

The development of inclusive practice

The post holder has a key role to play in developing and implementing inclusive barrier-free teaching and learning opportunities that raise standards of attainment, by enabling pupils with AEN to reach their optimum potential.

She/he should:

- contribute to supporting the school's inclusion policy;
- support teachers in enabling them to provide barrier-free teaching and learning opportunities that guarantee curriculum access for a diversity of pupils;
- contribute to monitoring and evaluating the impact of support, advice and training provided on educational inclusion;
- advise the Inclusion Coordinator on additional resources required to maximise inclusive practice.

Knowledge and understanding

She/he should:

- know the characteristics of a variety of effective teaching and learning styles to meet the needs of pupils with AEN;
- know and understand the principles of inclusive education;
- apply a range of inclusive education strategies to support AEN pupils and staff;
- use ICT and multimedia effectively to improve pupils' curriculum access and remove barriers to learning and participation;
- contribute to the professional development of other staff in relation to improving educational inclusion;
- support the planning, implementation and review of pupils' Inclusion Action Plans;
- be familiar with curriculum attainment targets and level descriptors;
- use appropriate and effective methods of communication;
- understand the need for appropriate confidentiality and professionalism.

Barrier-free learning

She/he should:

- support staff in identifying and providing effective teaching and learning approaches for pupils with AEN;
- assist in developing pupils' skills to learn more effectively;
- enable pupils with AEN to become more effective independent learners.

Pupil achievement

She/he should:

- support staff in understanding the learning needs of pupils with AEN;
- review the progress of supported AEN pupils with relevant staff.

Parent partnership

She/he should:

- contribute towards increasing parents' understanding and skills in supporting their child's learning at home.

Managing own performance and professional development

She/he should:

- prioritise and manage own time effectively;
- contribute to identifying own continuing professional development needs;
- use own initiative to problem solve;
- know when to withdraw support and consult with others;
- know how to respond positively in stressful and challenging circumstances;
- be able to work independently, and also as a member of an inclusion team;
- contribute to and participate in the annual school inclusion audit.

Appraisal of performance

The job description will be central to the annual process of reviewing continuing professional development. For this reason it is essential that the Learning Support Assistant fully understands and accepts the responsibilities specified.

Contract terms and duties

This job description forms part of the contract of employment of the person appointed to this post. It reflects the position at the present time only and may be reviewed in negotiation with the employee in the future.

© Rita Cheminais 2002

The Inclusion Coordinator, as line manager, will be responsible for the LSA's annual professional development review, as well as supporting their continuing professional development.

It is essential that everyone is clear about their role in moving inclusive educational practice forward within the school. For this reason, it is helpful if a brief outline of everyone's roles and responsibilities are made explicit to all staff. An example of a model brochure is included on the following pages. This could be distributed to all staff within a school.

High Hills School

Guidance on using
Learning Support Assistants

Introduction

High Hills School values and respects the contributions of the Learning Support Assistant (LSA) as a member of a whole-school collaborative teaching and learning team.

The LSA plays a crucial role in promoting barrier-free learning and participation opportunities for pupils with additional educational needs (AEN).

The effectiveness of the LSA is dependent on all teaching staff, pupils, parents, governors and the senior management team being clear about the role of the Learning Support Assistant in implementing and supporting the continuance of inclusive education for all pupils.

The LSA works in partnership with teachers and pupils in all key stages, both within and outside the school's OASIS Centre (Open Access Supporting Inclusive Study). Collaborative practice ensures that every child receives an entitlement to relevant, enjoyable, barrier-free learning experiences in a fully inclusive and secure school community.

In order to ensure the work of the Learning Support Assistant is effective, all teaching and pastoral staff, as well as pupils, must be clear about their role in supporting the LSA.

The following guidance is designed to provide a point of reference for all participants.

The role of the senior management team in supporting the LSA

- To provide a clear job description which is regularly reviewed, and gives details about the length of contract.

- To provide an appropriate induction programme.

- To provide opportunities for continuing professional development.

- To ensure the LSA is viewed as an integral resource within the school inclusion team, by teachers, pupils and their parents.

- To ensure the Inclusion Coordinator and all teaching staff fully understand the role of the LSA, and their own roles, in supporting the Learning Support Assistant.

- To ensure the LSA is included in relevant staff meetings and pupil-related meetings.

- To ensure procedures are in place for monitoring LSA effectiveness.

The role of the Inclusion Coordinator in supporting the LSA

- To oversee the induction programme of the LSA and provide clear guidelines of all expectations and responsibilities.

- To provide regular meeting time for LSAs to discuss inclusion issues.

- To provide information regarding AEN pupils' individual needs and targets.

- To provide the subject teachers with strategies to support the LSA in performing their duties.

- To check that planning time with subject teachers takes place.

- To ensure that LSAs keep up-to-date records of support.

- To identify the training needs of LSAs and make the appropriate provision for this.

- To include LSAs in any relevant reviews concerning AEN pupils supported.

- To treat the LSA as a valued member of an inclusive teaching and learning team.

The role of the subject teacher in supporting the LSA

- To accept the LSA as a team member, particularly when working within the classroom.

- To take overall responsibility for addressing AEN pupils' needs.

- To deploy the LSA efficiently and effectively, making expectations and responsibilities clear, when assigning tasks.

- To encourage the LSA to use their own initiative, talents and skills.

- To be aware of potential difficulties the LSA may face, and be willing to communicate if a problem occurs.

- To promote inclusion, using the LSA with pupils.

- Where possible, to include the LSA in lesson planning.

- To provide adequate time for any advance curriculum differentiation by the LSA, for pupils with AEN.

- To give LSA feedback on pupil progress and the effectiveness of their support.

The role of the LSA

- To carry out tasks assigned by the Inclusion Coordinator.

- To keep records of support given to AEN pupils, while being aware of maintaining confidentiality.

- To be flexible and able to adapt in both task and approach, to meet the individual needs of the pupils.

- To develop a sensitive, empathic and inclusive understanding of pupils' needs.

- To be clear about objectives and methods of working that promote barrier-free learning opportunities.

- To help promote pupils' self-esteem and motivation, empowering them to take responsibility for their own learning.

- To promote peer acceptance of educational inclusion.

- To attend meetings and training sessions as required.

- To work with staff in removing barriers to learning.

- To act as a responsible member of staff, with respect to pupils, staff and resources.

- To extend pupils' learning.

Teaching Assistants (TAs) make a significant contribution to inclusion by increasing the capacity of schools to respond to pupil diversity. They help children to learn alongside their peers by facilitating participation and learning, building confidence, self-esteem and independence, to enable the child to reach their full potential.

OFSTED (2002) in an evaluation of the impact of TAs commented:

> They are making a valuable contribution to the teaching of literacy and numeracy through the support they provide for pupils, including through the intervention and catch-up programmes associated with the NLNS. (OFSTED 2002c: 64)

CSIE (2001) identified aspects of learning supporters' (TAs') work:

> They help to prevent and overcome barriers to learning arising from the interaction between the school environment, a range of individual impairments, as well as social and economic factors. Their work involves academic, physical, social and communication aspects of learning. They are involved in teaching, caring, counselling, facilitating communication and curriculum adaptation and reform. (Shaw 2001: 4)

The quality of teaching improves when the TA works in close partnership with the teacher. The quality of teaching is also improved when the TA:

- is clear about their role and expectations;
- knows how to give feedback on pupils' learning and behaviour;
- generates more challenging discussions with pupils during learning support;
- has sufficient subject knowledge to challenge and extend pupils' learning;
- utilises good questioning skills;
- enables the teacher to use a wider range of teaching methods;
- enables the teacher to match work more precisely to pupils' different abilities;
- can manage the behaviour of pupils they are working with.

Quality trained TAs help to raise standards in the primary phase by:

- understanding children's needs and their behaviour;
- interacting effectively with pupils to promote their learning;
- assessing where pupils are in their learning and what they need to do to make further progress.

Inclusive schools will need to monitor the time some pupils spend with TAs on a daily basis. OFSTED notes:

> Some schools may be unaware that some pupils of lower ability or with SEN spend too much time with teaching assistants and do not receive enough skilled training from a qualified teacher. (OFSTED 2002c: 44)

CSIE in their report on learning supporters and inclusion, records the following comment from an assistant:

> The teacher looks at you and thinks there is the LSA. Let them get on with it. They have hardly any contact with the child. That is not inclusion. That is putting the child at the edge.   (Shaw 2001: 11)

OFSTED (2002c) recommends primary schools should:

- monitor the pattern of TAs work throughout the school;
- establish appraisal systems for TAs;
- ensure that the level of practical and administrative support for teachers does not diminish as TAs provide more teaching and learning support in lessons.

OFSTED will continue to monitor the impact of TAs, the quality of their work, their training and appraisal.

The number of TAs employed in primary schools continues to increase. Head teachers are advised to consider creating a post of senior or lead TA, who would be responsible for managing the work of other TAs in the school.

Similarly, the LEA should consider recruiting a TA Coordinator who will lead the support, training and development of TAs, throughout the authority.

Managing inclusion at an operational level

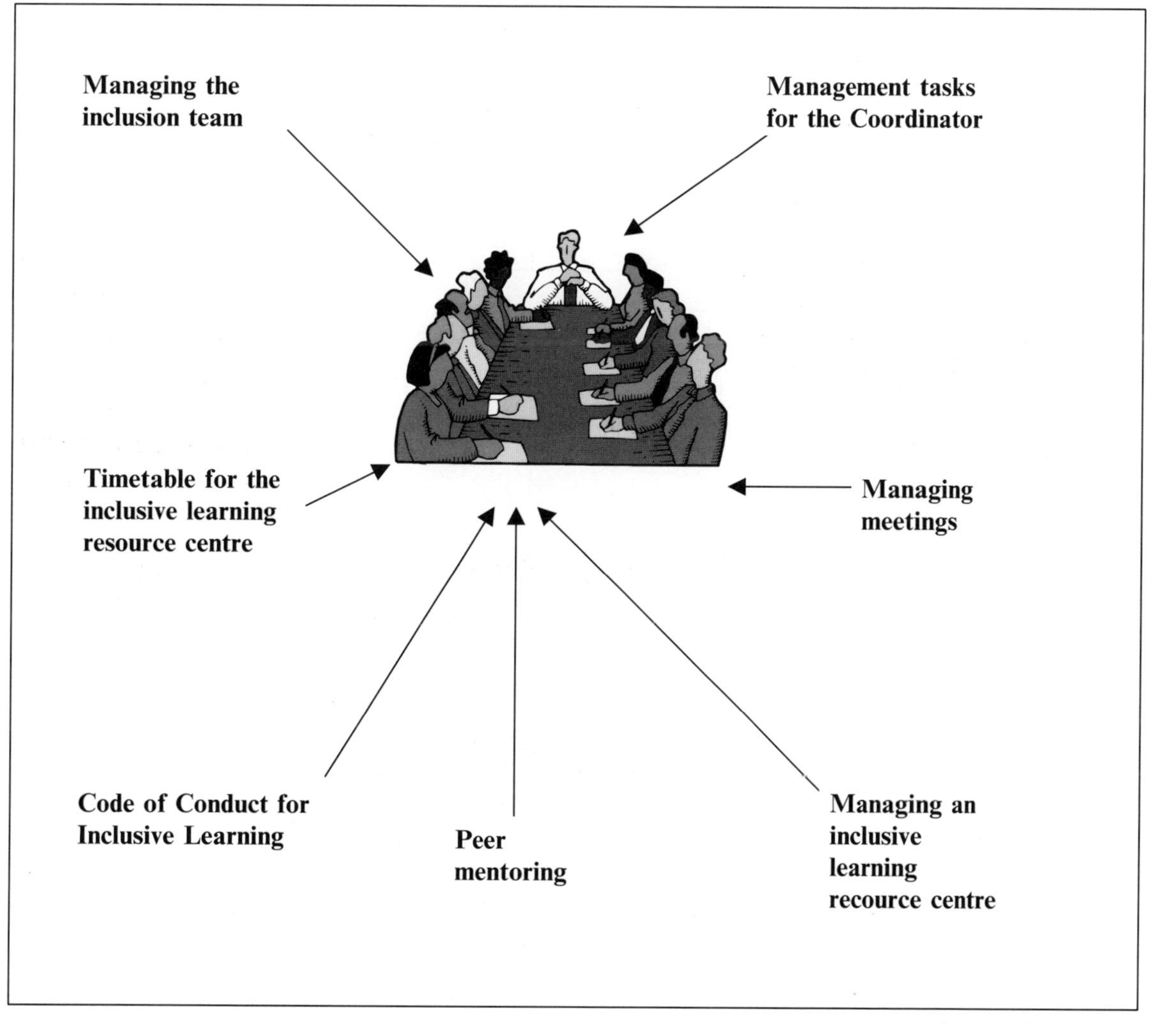

Management involves getting things done through others, by others, together with others and in spite of others. The Inclusion Coordinator as team leader will want to ensure that every member of the inclusion team has the opportunity to demonstrate their strengths, skills and abilities.

The core members of the inclusion team will comprise the Inclusion Coordinator, Inclusion teacher and LSAs assigned to a particular key stage.

The inclusion team will function best in a collaborative culture, with a high level of trust and openness, and where the Inclusion Coordinator is committed to the development of each team member. Such empowerment and participation among the team can help inclusion move forward, at a faster pace, within the school.

The inclusion team will liaise and meet with key participants, as outlined in the Figure 2.1 flow chart. The management framework illustrated below, although a secondary school model, can be applied to a range of educational settings.

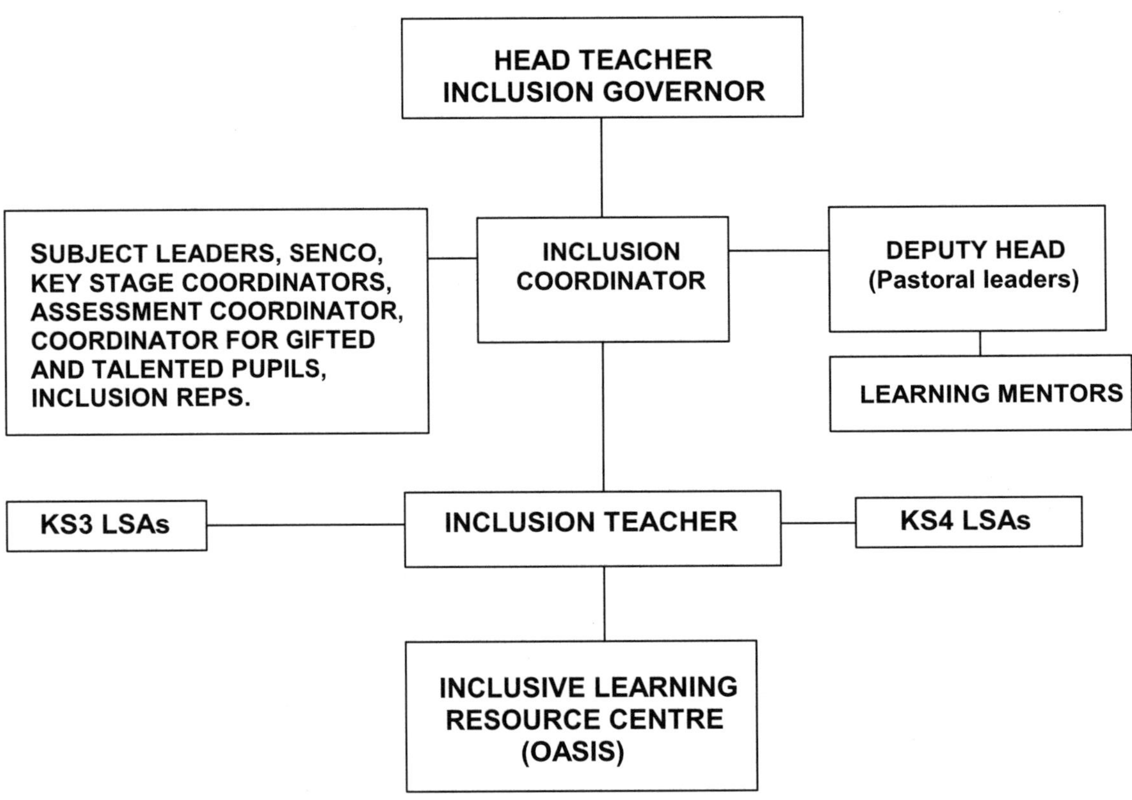

Figure 2.1: Management framework supporting the core inclusion team.

© Rita Cheminais 2002

24

Successful teamwork depends on aims and objectives being made clear, and members working together on the basis of:

- a common purpose and goal
- agreed procedures
- shared vision, perceptions and values
- commitment and involvement
- cooperation and collaboration
- open discussion and consultation
- recognition and praise
- listening to each other
- regular review and reflection.

The Inclusion Coordinator as team leader needs to:

> . . . deal sensitively with people, recognising individual needs and take account of these in securing a consistent team approach to raising achievement . . . (TTA 1998: 7)

A successful inclusion team is flexible and creative, and thrives on team achievements, rather than on isolated separate individual achievements.

People management may not always run smoothly, and the Inclusion Coordinator needs to employ strategies that will reduce conflict and resistance to change.

Three tips for diffusing conflict are:

- Listen to what is said, show your concern, understanding and empathy, and ask questions in respect of what they wish to see happen.
- Give those who disrupt meetings a task to complete, e.g. taking the minutes or distributing handouts.
- Alternatively, listen to their viewpoint, thank them for their contribution and quickly invite others into the discussion.

Managing meetings

Ensuring meetings are effective and making efficient use of team members' and others' time is important, especially in relation to maintaining the good will and commitment of participants.

Illustrated on page 26 is an example of best practice of a Coordinator's meeting schedule. Schools are at liberty to adapt such a rigorous programme of meetings for inclusion, to fit into their particular context, in relation to national and local priorities, as well as taking account of the political climate.

Example of a meeting schedule for inclusion

1. Monday morning briefing with inclusion team to check through the week's programme and timetable, and update team members on any significant events or changes that will impact on the work of the team.

2. Provide the opportunity for members of the inclusion team to refer any urgent issues of concern back to the Inclusion Coordinator at the end of the school day. This could be done face-to-face or via email.

3. Fortnightly timetabled inclusion team meeting, to review progress, raise issues, generate ideas.

4. Fortnightly timetabled meeting between the Inclusion Coordinator and the SMT to feed back on progress and report any inclusion issues raised at team level.

5. Monthly or half-termly meeting which includes the inclusion representatives from subject departments, Key Stage Coordinators, SENCO, Strategy Managers, Coordinator for Gifted and Talented Pupils, Assessment Coordinator.

6. Monthly or half-termly meeting with pastoral leaders, heads of year, Learning Mentors, Counsellors, any relevant external professionals, e.g. educational psychologist, education welfare officer, Connexions Personal Adviser.

7. A meeting once a term between the Inclusion Coordinator and the inclusion governor, to provide updates on developments, and progress reports.

8. Annual meeting with the school's Link Adviser, or General Adviser/ Consultant for Inclusion.

Management tasks for the Inclusion Coordinator

Management action	Coordinator tasks	Input to inclusion team members	Support for individuals in team
Define goals	Clarify goals Establish timescale Gather information Identify resources	Assemble team Explain goals and rationale Generate commitment Encourage questions	Check individuals understand goals Respond to questions/concerns Ensure individual involvement
Plan and direct	Identify options Investigate how to make best use of team members' skills Plan timing of events Check resources needed Identify success criteria Generate plan ownership	Consult with team members Brainstorm ideas List suggestions Agree priorities	Listen to suggestions Identify/assess individual abilities Coach relevant skills as required
Organise and brief	Establish procedures Draw up brief and action plan Check individual understanding of roles and tasks Listen to and respond to feedback	Set up appropriate structures and agree on sub-tasks Communicate agreed plan Take questions and queries Delegate tasks/responsibilities Finalise plan	Check understanding of individual roles Reward commitment and enthusiasm Reward good ideas Invite feedback
Control, support and monitor	Report progress at agreed intervals to key stakeholders Amend action plan, if necessary Set examples Maintain commitment to goals	Coordinate work of subgroups Check resources are in use Provide feedback on tasks Deal with conflicts/disagreements Celebrate sub-goal achievement Resolve emergent problems	Provide support to individuals Encourage disclosure of problems Recognise individual achievements Reassure where necessary Check agreed deadlines are on course
Evaluate and review	Evaluate goal achievement by applying agreed success criteria Report on team performance Consider future action Note potential improvements	Give feedback on achievement Invite team to review their effectiveness Identify learning/insights gained	Provide individual feedback on goal achievement Recognise individual development Recognise contributions made to the team Gather individual perceptions of team's effectiveness

Source: West (1995: 84)

Although the example schedule for meetings may appear rather excessive, if a school is really committed to raising standards in teaching and learning, which will impact on improving inclusive classroom practice, then key members of staff driving inclusion need to be given the necessary quality time and support to meet and discuss issues, and share best practice.

Effective meetings are those where all participants attending are clear about the purpose and function of the meeting. For example, is the meeting to give and receive information, to consult, to monitor and evaluate progress, make decisions, generate ideas, problem solve, motivate and foster commitment or plan and allocate responsibilities? It is also a good management strategy to separate strategic discussions from meetings dealing with operational matters.

Meeting checklist

- ☐ Prepare the meeting agenda in advance, and invite items to be added from participants beforehand.

- ☐ Prepare any necessary briefing or discussion papers, and distribute prior to the meeting.

- ☐ Invite, or allocate on a rotational basis, a person to take minutes at the meeting.

- ☐ Always review the action points from the previous meeting first.

- ☐ Clarify the purpose of the meeting.

- ☐ Keep to the agenda, and try to limit the number of items discussed to no more than five or six items.

- ☐ Keep to the time frame established for the length of the meeting.

- ☐ Encourage participation from all members present.

- ☐ If 'any other business' is likely to overrun, then recommend that the issue is placed on the agenda for the next meeting.

- ☐ Take a vote to check consensus on any key decisions.

- ☐ Summarise the main points or outcomes at the close of the meeting.

- ☐ Set the date and time for the next meeting, if it is not already pre-planned.

- ☐ Ensure minutes of the meeting are typed up and distributed as soon as possible following the meeting, and that those unable to attend the meeting receive a copy.

- ☐ Retain a copy of the minutes from each meeting on file for future reference.

- ☐ Ensure any outcomes from meetings that will impact on whole-school policy and inclusive provision are publicised to all staff in the appropriate manner, bearing in mind confidentiality.

Record of the meeting of: ____

Date of meeting: ____________________________ **Time:** ____________________________

Agenda items:

1.

2.

3.

4.

5.

6.

AOB

Significant outcomes or matters arising from the meeting:

Date and time of next meeting: ____

Minutes recorded by: ____

Meeting closed at: ____________________________

The Inclusion Coordinator will oversee the strategic management of the school's inclusive learning resource centre (ILRC). A full-time inclusion teacher and an LSA will staff the centre on a daily basis. A team of LSAs will also work outside the centre, across the curriculum, with a diversity of targeted pupils.

The location of the centre should be an integral part of the main school building, preferably attached to, or part of, the existing school library or ICT suite, and on the ground floor to ensure access for those with physical disabilities. It needs to have state-of-the-art technology, to support barrier-free learning and participation. For example, the centre or suite should house sufficient ICT hardware with internet access; provide a range of portable laptop computers for use outside the centre in classrooms; a good selection of desktop publishing programmes; a Power Point facility; a range of digital cameras and camcorders; Smart boards/interactive white boards; television video/DVD players to enable videoconferencing to occur, within and outside the school centre; as well as provide a range of hand-held audio recorders/players; basic reference books, linked to the curriculum; in fact, resources that enable the centre to become a 'Virtual Learning Centre'.

The centre should be furnished to facilitate individual and group learning activities, for the full ability range of pupils, as well as to support relaxation, and brain gym/accelerated learning activities. For senior managers, it may be an issue of relocating some ICT learning resources, or extending the function and purpose of the school's existing library/ICT suite to include more multimedia learning facilities.

Schools may wish to give the centre a more user-friendly title, and I suggest choosing something inclusive to meet a diversity of needs, such as, the OASIS Centre, which stands for Open Access Supporting Inclusive Study. Electronic registration to enter OASIS would enable a check to be kept on those using the centre, which includes staff as well as pupils/students.

The centre needs to be innovative and experimental in its approach to supporting barrier-free learning and inclusion. For example, OASIS using videoconferencing to model inclusive teaching and learning approaches that can be relayed to staff/classrooms throughout the school, and in other schools, is a good approach to presenting a whole-school staff INSET on inclusion.

OASIS will operate before, during and after school hours in order to respond flexibly to the needs of a diversity of users. In view of the extended role of the centre, staff working in OASIS must be recompensed either with additional payment or time-in-lieu for the extra hours they devote to supporting and improving inclusive learning.

OASIS checklist

☐ The purpose and aims of the centre are known to all staff and pupils.

☐ OASIS entry and exit criteria and procedures are made explicit.

☐ The Inclusion Coordinator acts as gatekeeper for referrals to the centre.

☐ The OASIS Centre Code of Conduct for Inclusive Learning is understood by all.

☐ The weekly timetable for OASIS is publicised to staff and pupils.

☐ No more than 12 pupils will work within the centre at any one time.

☐ A maximum of six weeks intervention from OASIS and the inclusion team will be made available to extend learning and/or support behaviour.

☐ All pupils and staff using the centre must register electronically each time they visit OASIS.

☐ Requests to loan technological resources to support inclusive learning must be lodged with the inclusion teacher in OASIS.

☐ Staff and pupils borrowing equipment from the centre will be responsible for ensuring that it is returned in good condition and in full working order.

☐ The roles of the LSAs, inclusion teacher and the Inclusion Coordinator are known by all staff and pupils.

☐ The Inclusion Coordinator will be available at the beginning and end of each school day to deal with any inclusion issues arising.

☐ Pupils receiving intervention and support from the inclusion team, within and outside the OASIS Centre, will have their progress tracked and monitored by the Inclusion Coordinator.

☐ Staff visiting and utilising the centre's resources will be expected to contribute evidence of improvement, in their inclusive classroom practice, to the Inclusion Coordinator.

☐ The Inclusion Coordinator will report regularly to the SMT/inclusion governor, on the effectiveness of the work of the inclusion team and the OASIS Centre.

Code of Conduct for Inclusive Learning

This is a barrier-free learning zone.

Follow this Code at all times.

- [ ] **It's cool to learn**

- [ ] **Everyone is good at something**

- [ ] **It's OK to make mistakes – we all learn from them**

- [ ] **Every learner is worth the time**

- [ ] **The best learners ask questions**

- [ ] **Learn to take responsibility for your own learning**

- [ ] **To learn and remember anything, see it, hear it and do it**

- [ ] **If you can dream it, you can do it. Believe in yourself**

- [ ] **Never, never give up trying**

- [ ] **Everything is possible**

- [ ] **Always give that little bit extra effort**

- [ ] **Success comes in cans, not in can'ts**

- [ ] **Never put anyone down because they can't do something**

- [ ] **Respect each other's preferred learning style**

- [ ] **Ask yourself the question, 'What have you learned today?'**

A model timetable for an inclusive learning resource centre

	Monday	Tuesday	Wednesday	Thursday	Friday
8.00–8.30 a.m.	Inclusion Coordinator and OASIS teacher meet to review weekly inclusion programme	Brain gym session for pupils and subject staff	Improving study skills session for pupils and subject staff	Accelerated learning techniques session for pupils and subject staff	Mind-mapping and memory technqiues session for pupils and subject staff
9.15–10.45 a.m.	Pupil support for learning and subject teacher access for curriculum differentiation	Pupil support for learning and subject teacher access for curriculum differentiation	Pupil support for learning and subject teacher access for curriculum differentiation	Pupil support for learning and subject teacher access for curriculum differentiation	Pupil support for learning and subject teacher access for curriculum differentiation
11.00–12.00 a.m.	As above	As above	As above	As above	As above
12.00–1.00 p.m.	Study support KS3 pupils	Study support KS4 pupils	Study support KS3 pupils	Study support KS4 pupils	Staff drop-in session on inclusion queries
1.30–2.30 p.m.	Pupil support to enrich and extend learning. Support with curriculum differentiation	Pupil support to enrich and extend learning. Support with curriculum differentiation	Pupil support to enrich and extend learning. Support with curriculum differentiation	Pupil support to enrich and extend learning. Support with curriculum differentiation	SMT meeting with Inclusion Coordinator
2.30–3.30 p.m.	As above	As above	As above	As above	Inclusion team meeting
4.00–5.30 p.m.	Thinking Club for pupils	Workshop on learning styles for staff	Parent/carers workshop on using ICT to support their child's learning	Staff workshop on Accelerated Learning Techniques	Closed

The Code of Conduct for Inclusive Learning would ideally be laminated and displayed in all classrooms, as well as in the OASIS Centre. The Code would have been negotiated and agreed with all pupils and staff. It reflects the inclusive philosophy that teaching and learning, achievements, attitudes and the well-being of every pupil matter.

The above examples of activities would be on a half-termly rolling programme, for staff and pupils, according to the identified priorities for improving inclusive learning. It may be necessary for the inclusion team to target one subject department at a time, or an aspect of a subject, in relation to supporting staff in improving curriculum differentiation for a diversity of pupils, within the full ability range.

Peer mentoring to support learning

The Inclusion Coordinator is best placed to recruit, train, organise and manage older pupils acting as peer mentors or 'study buddies' to younger pupils, particularly upon transition to the next key stage or phase of education. This is also a very positive inclusion initiative, which encourages pupils to take greater responsibility for their own learning and that of others.

At the beginning of each academic year, the Inclusion Coordinator will issue an advertisement to targeted year groups, inviting volunteers to become study buddies to younger pupils.

Interested volunteers will complete a simple questionnaire and application form, and return this to the Inclusion Coordinator within a week. All applications will be considered, and after taking into account the prospective study buddies' record of attendance, punctuality, reliability and work record, suitable volunteers will be chosen and their parents/carers will be informed by letter. Unsuccessful volunteers will be sent a letter of thanks regarding their application and expression of interest.

An initial meeting will be set up with selected study buddies. The Inclusion Coordinator will outline the commitment required and the content of the training sessions. Study buddies will be provided with a guidance booklet and an agreement to sign. Their parents/carers will also sign the agreement, as well as the Inclusion Coordinator.

Study buddies will undertake the minimum of four compulsory training sessions, delivered by the Inclusion Coordinator and members of their inclusion team. Additional optional training sessions will be offered to study buddies as appropriate. The training will adopt a practical approach as to how to support and develop pupils' study skills, deliver homework support, build self-confidence, utilise appropriate listening skills, make decisions and solve problems.

Upon the successful completion of training, study buddies will be allocated a younger pupil who is experiencing difficulties with study generally, or who has requested study support or mentoring for a particular subject area.

The Inclusion Coordinator will monitor the progress of the study buddy, and of the pupil being supported each week. When the pupil being supported by a study buddy gains the confidence and skills to become an independent learner, their study buddy will be allocated to another pupil requiring similar support.

At the end of the academic year, study buddies will receive a Certificate of Study Support, which can be placed in their individual Record of Achievement.

Study Buddy Guide

Introduction

A **study buddy** acts as a guide, adviser and trusted friend to younger pupils who are having difficulties with their work, with aspects of school life or in making friends.

If you can spare some time every week to support a pupil with their homework, help them to develop their study skills and improve their self-confidence, and you are willing to undertake some basic training, then this guide will outline the study buddy scheme.

If you want to find out more about becoming a study buddy, then visit Mr Fraser the Inclusion Coordinator in the OASIS Centre.

Becoming a study buddy for a year will enable you to obtain a Certificate of Study Support, which will be added to your Record of Achievement. It will also give you the experience of taking on a position of responsibility.

What qualities are needed to become a study buddy?

- Good attendance at school
- A good time keeper
- The ability to work with other pupils
- Show interest and ability in study and curriculum subjects
- Good listening skills
- Sensitivity and understanding
- Know how to give support and guidance to other pupils
- Willing to give up a lunch-time or some time after school
- Approachable
- Reliable

Why become a study buddy?

- Help others to improve their study skills

- Increase the self-confidence of those you support

- Offer friendship

- Set a good example as a 'model' student

- Learn to respect differences in others

- Help younger pupils to solve problems, make decisions and share worries

- Develop awareness about others' study difficulties

- Gain experience in taking on extra responsibility

What sort of support will you offer pupils?

- Help with homework or course work

- Assist pupils in improving their study skills

- Advise on how to tackle a subject or piece of work

- Help with revision of work for a test

- Help pupils to use ICT to support study

- Help some pupils understand technical words or difficult text

© Rita Cheminais 2002

STUDY BUDDY AGREEMENT

I agree to:

be on time for training and pupil support sessions

be available for one lunch-time or after-school
session per week

maintain confidentiality

work cooperatively

treat others with equal respect

accept advice and guidance from staff

attend study buddy meetings

feed back to Inclusion Coordinator on progress and
concerns

Study buddy signature: _______________________________

Parent/carer signature: _______________________________

Inclusion Coordinator signature: _____________________

Date: _______________________________

School self-evaluation supporting inclusion

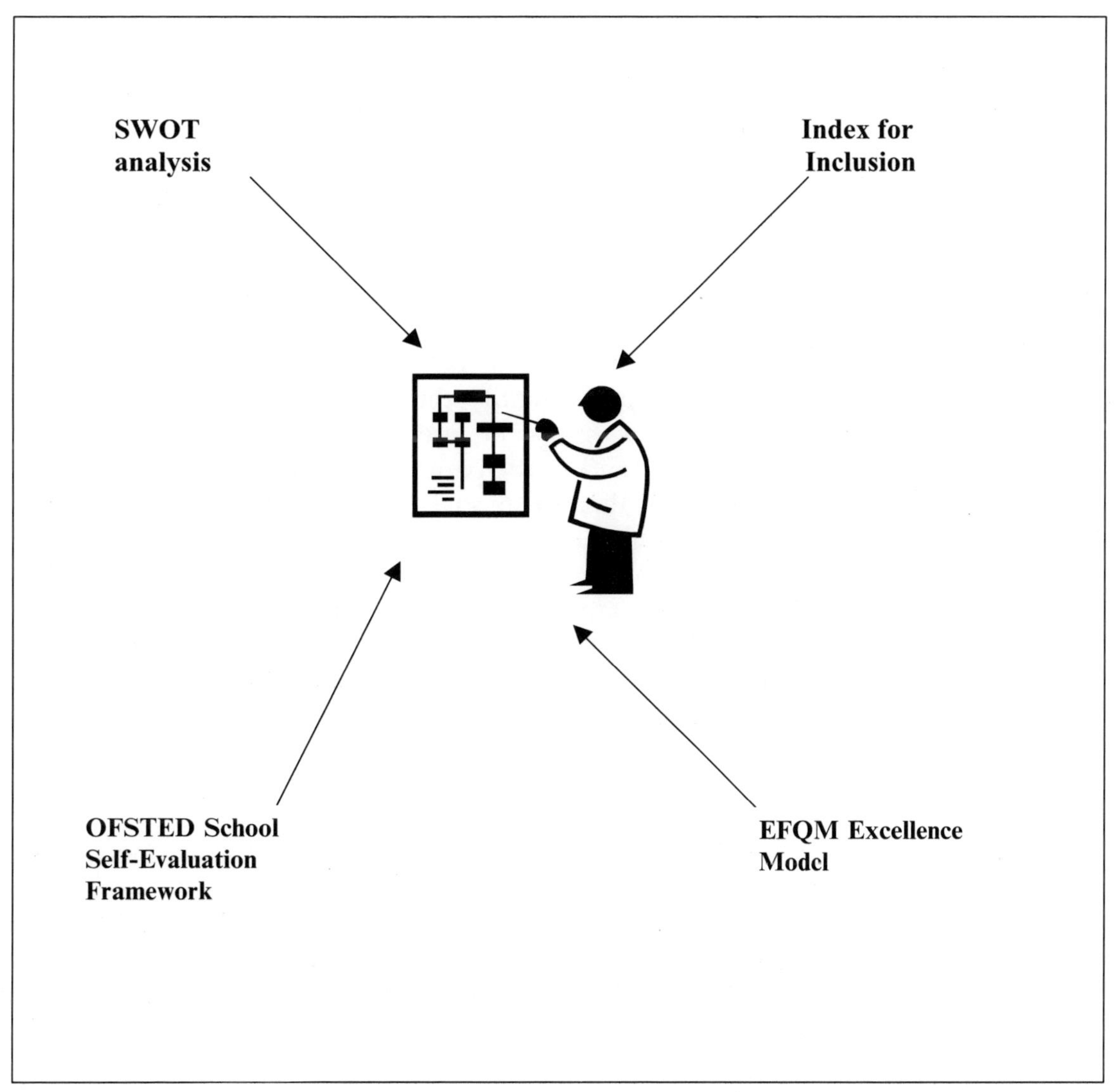

If schools are to maintain high standards and secure improvement in inclusive educational practice, they need a framework or model with which to appraise their own performance, and to monitor and evaluate effective teaching and learning.

While a model of school self-evaluation should support the four principles of best value known as the four Cs (compare, challenge, consult and compete), it is up to the self-managing school to select the evaluation approach that best suits their own particular context.

In view of this factor, no single model will be promoted to support the improvement of inclusive education. However, three recognised credible frameworks are outlined, which describe how they can be applied to supporting inclusive practice in schools.

The three models are as follows:

- the Index for Inclusion
- the European Foundation for Quality Management (EFQM) Excellence Model
- the OFSTED School Self-Evaluation Model

Whichever model is selected to support inclusive education in schools, the main purposes will be:

- to involve the whole school community in the improvement process;
- to improve the quality of education for all pupils;
- to promote and share best inclusive practice with others.

The common advantage to all the three models is that they engage all stakeholders in a crucial development activity that strengthens a corporate consensual understanding of what inclusive education and barrier-free learning and participation opportunities entail. All three models help to identify the longer-term inclusive education improvements necessary in order to foster high achievement, increase learning and participation for all pupils. Many schools by utilising a self-evaluation model find it helpful in analysing what they do, determining priorities for change and putting the identified priorities into practice.

School self-evaluation is about reflection on concerns related to inclusion, which assist in establishing criteria for improvement, and determine the most appropriate methods to evaluate the outcomes and impact of barrier-free teaching and learning.

*SWOT
analysis*

Before evaluating inclusive culture, policy and provision using one of the three recommended models of school self-evaluation, a useful starting point is to undertake a SWOT analysis. This will identify the strengths, weaknesses, opportunities and threats existing in the school, which will promote or inhibit improvement in educational inclusion.

SWOT analysis

Inclusion issue to be addressed

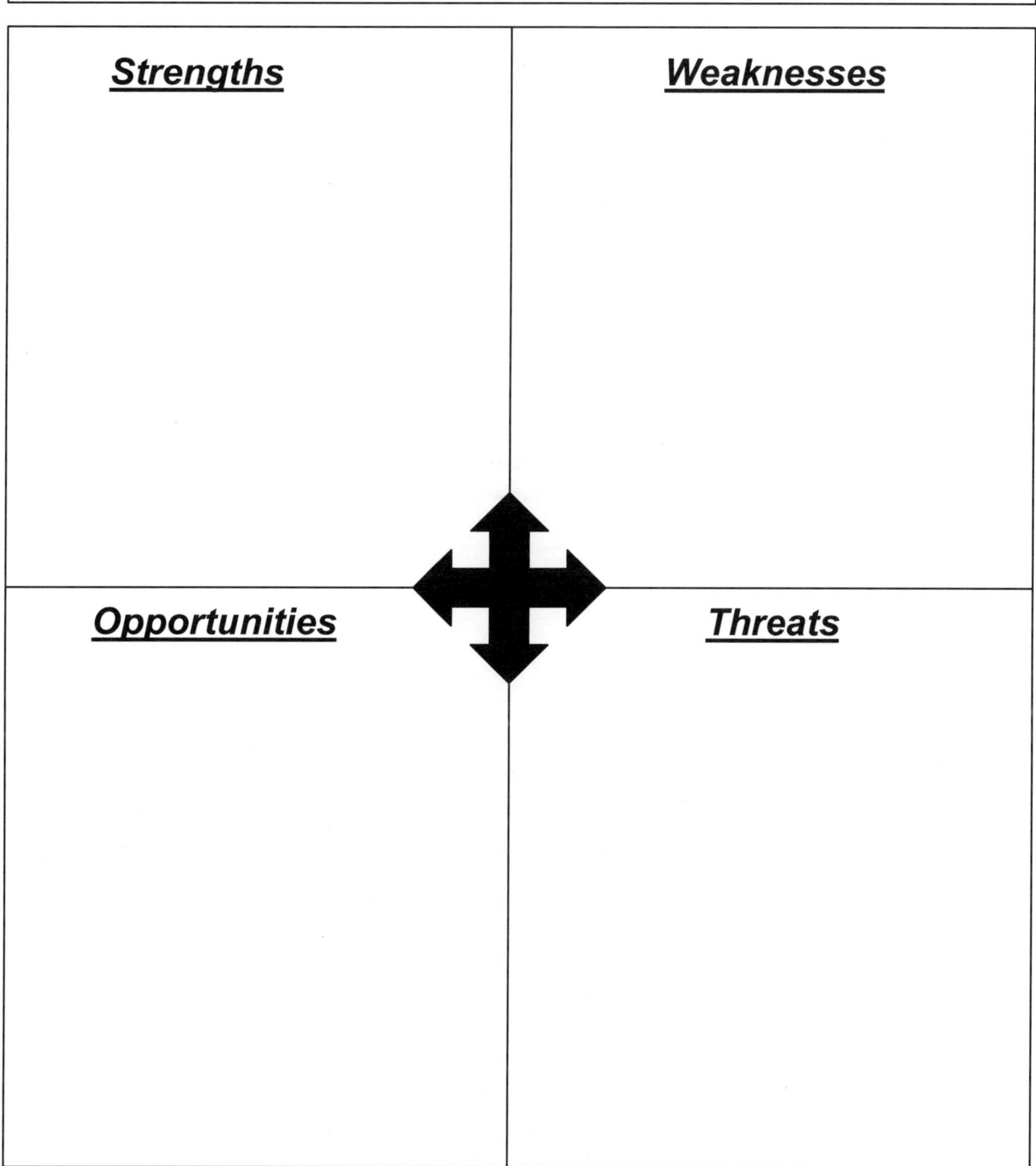

Part 2 of the Index for Inclusion describes how the Index can contribute to the development of inclusion, by informing school self-review and improvement planning.

The Index process comprises five phases, which are outlined in Figure 3.1, with the school improvement planning cycle shown in italics.

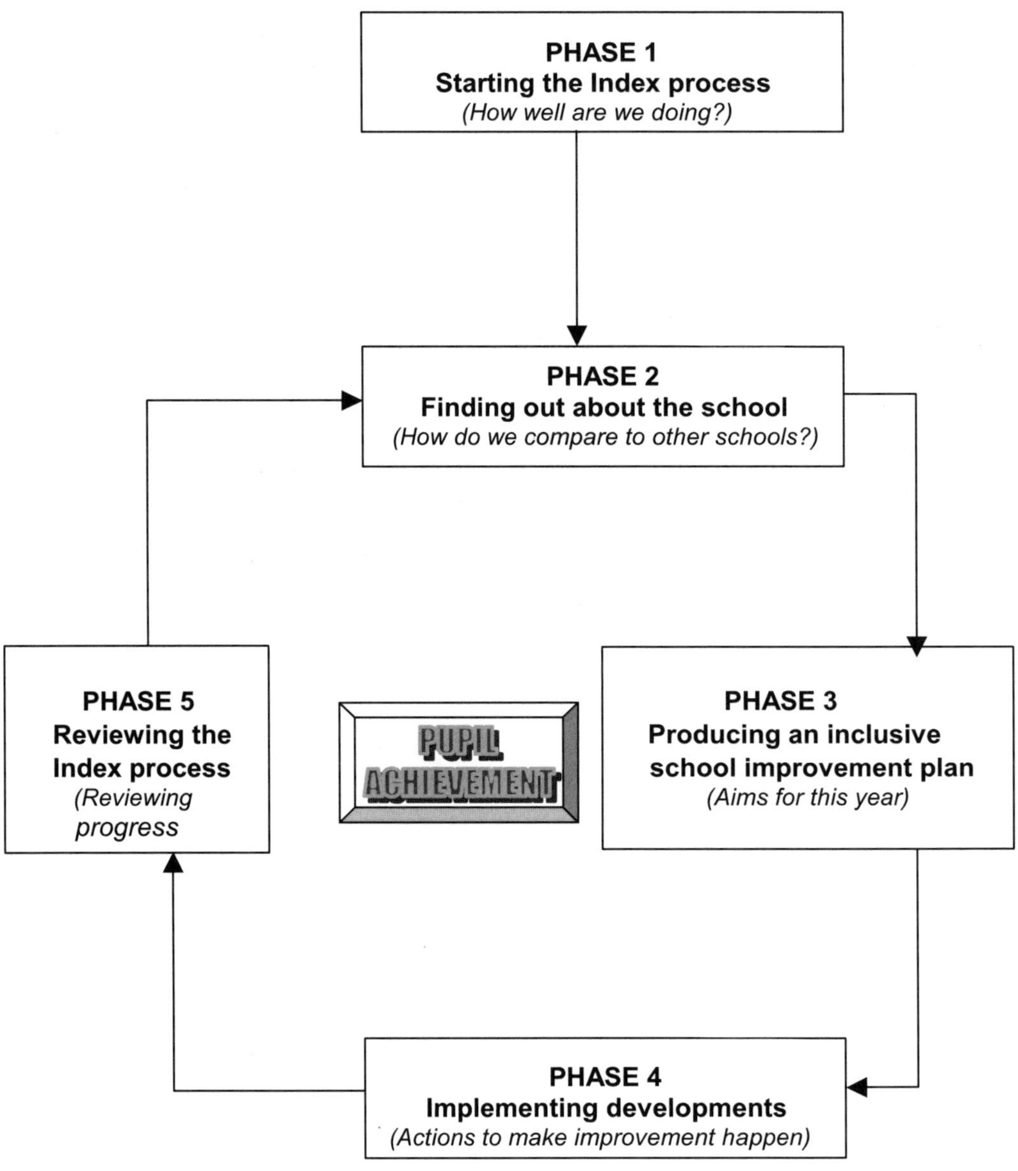

Figure 3.1: The Index process and the school improvement planning cycle

The Index for Inclusion

Phase 1: Starting the inclusion process

- Establish a coordinating group for inclusion within the school
- Raise whole-school awareness about the purpose and value of the Index
- Coordinating group to reflect upon their own knowledge of barriers to learning and participation, and inclusion
- Coordinating group to prioritise the use of selected indicators and questions related to inclusive culture, policy and practice
- Coordinating group to decide who to involve as the other participants

Phase 2: Finding out about the school's current knowledge about inclusion

- Exploring the knowledge of staff and governors via an INSET day
- Exploring the knowledge of pupils via questionnaire as part of PSHE
- Exploring the knowledge of parents/carers and community members via questionnaire, focus groups
- Deciding inclusion priorities following an analysis of the consultation evidence

Phase 3: Producing an inclusive school improvement plan

- Applying the Index process to the formulation of the school improvement plan
- Putting agreed inclusion priorities into the school improvement plan, specifying timescales, resources, staff development, monitoring procedures and success criteria

Phase 4: Implementing inclusive developments

- Putting inclusion priorities into practice, which may require further exploration using dimensions, indicators and questions from the Index
- Sustaining development, particularly in relation to collaborative work, sharing best practice and expertise, providing mutual staff support, listening to the opinions of staff and communicating progress in meeting priorities
- Recording the progress made in educational inclusion, and judging this against the success criteria outlined in the school improvement plan

---

Phase 5: Reviewing the Index process

- Evaluating developments in relation to school inclusion culture, policy and practice; reflect on changes and consider future improvements/developments
- Reviewing the way the Index has been used with a critical friend, to challenge school practices, and to decide how it has helped the school to adopt a greater commitment to inclusion
- Continuing to use the Index process to complement the annual school improvement planning cycle
- Re-examining aspects of inclusive school culture, policy and practice, using relevant indicators and questions from the Index

  (New staff joining the school must be made familiar with the Index process and understand how it informs their own inclusive classroom practice.)

© Rita Cheminais 2002

The pages following deal with Inclusive Cultures, Inclusive Policies and Inclusive Practices. The six boxed headings within them provide the inclusion aspects to focus on in the school improvement plan.

The modified indicators (adapted from the Index for Inclusion) under each heading, provide targets/priorities for further action. The selection of these will be governed by how far the school is already developing inclusion.

Inclusive Cultures

Building an inclusive community

To make everyone feel more welcome

To develop a culture where pupils help each other

To strengthen staff collaboration

To improve mutual respect between staff and pupils

To strengthen partnership between staff and parents

To foster staff/governor closer working relationships

To increase local community involvement with school

Establishing inclusive values

To raise expectations for all pupils

To ensure all share a common inclusion philosophy

To ensure all pupils are equally valued

To heighten staff/pupils' inclusion role

To enable staff to remove all barriers to learning

To minimise discriminatory practices

Inclusive Policies

Developing a school for all

To make fair staff appointments/promotions

To ensure new staff are settled into the school

To admit a diversity of pupils from the community

To make school buildings physically accessible

To help new pupils settle into the school

To arrange teaching groups to value diversity

Organising support for diversity

To coordinate all forms of support

To ensure staff CPD responds to pupil diversity

To ensure SEN policy is an inclusion policy

To ensure SEN COP reduces barriers to learning

To coordinate EAL and learning support

To link pastoral/behaviour support policies to curriculum development/learning support policies

To decrease the number of exclusions

To reduce barriers to school attendance

To minimise bullying

© Rita Cheminais 2002

48

Inclusive Practices

Orchestrating learning

To make lessons more responsive to pupil diversity

To make lessons more accessible to all pupils

To ensure lessons develop understanding of difference

To ensure pupils become more actively involved in their own learning

To ensure pupils learn collaboratively, across the curriculum

To ensure assessment encourages the achievement of all pupils

To ensure classroom discipline is based on mutual respect

To ensure teachers plan, review and teach in partnership more regularly

To ensure teachers support the learning and participation of all pupils

To ensure LSAs support the learning and participation of all pupils

To ensure homework contributes to the learning of all pupils

To ensure all pupils have the opportunity to partake in extra-curricular activities

Mobilising resources

To ensure school resources are distributed fairly to support inclusion

To ensure community resources are drawn upon

To ensure staff expertise is fully utilised

To ensure pupil difference is used as a resource for teaching and learning

To ensure staff develop resources to support learning and participation

The European Foundation for Quality Management (EFQM) Excellence Model is based on a framework of nine generic criteria, which are equally relevant to schools.

This model is broader then the OFSTED inspection framework, in that it provides a vehicle for schools to gauge the quality of their educational provision, particularly in relation to teaching and learning, and inclusion. It also provides more directly for a self-assessment approach, and improvement activity.

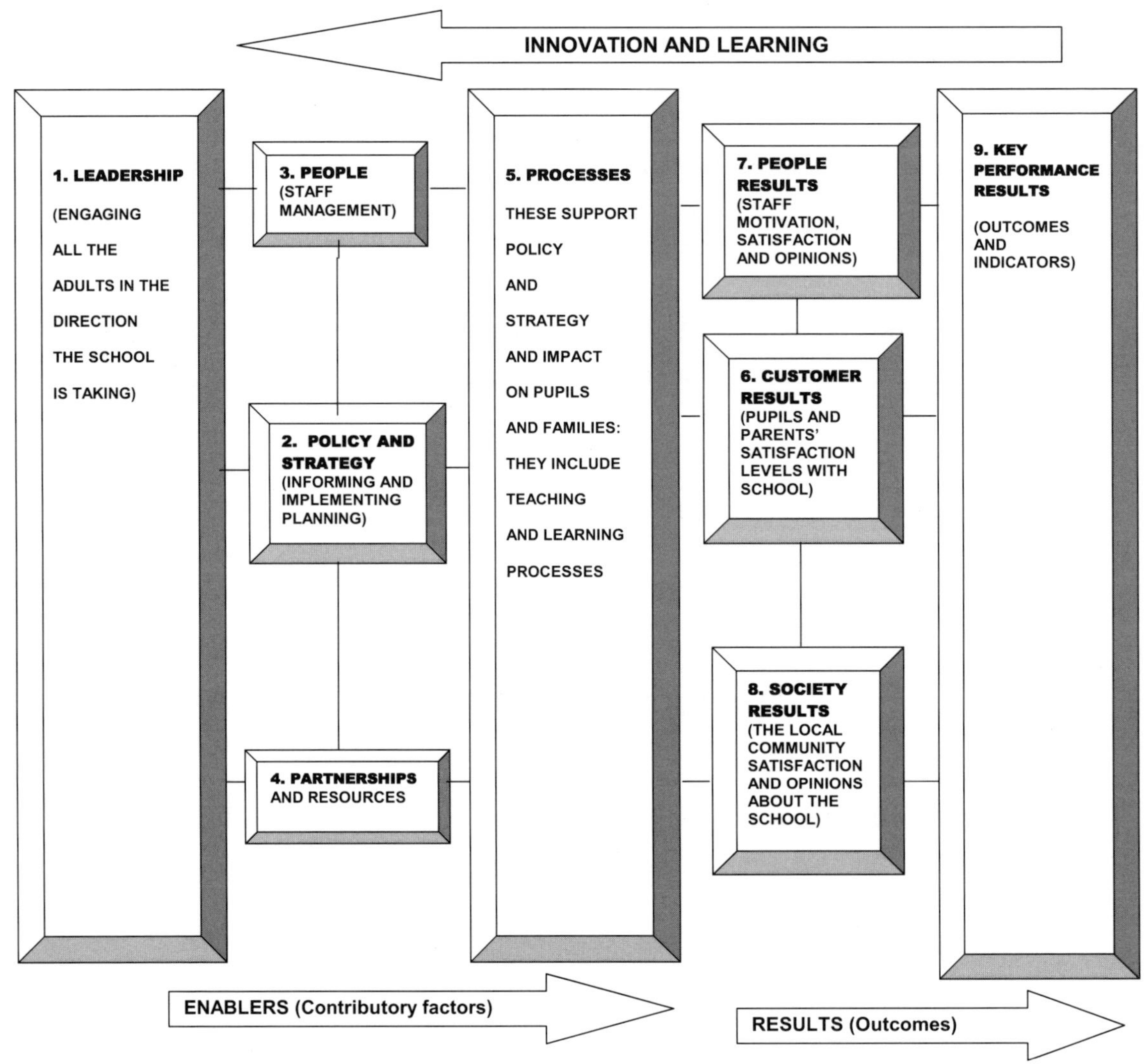

® EFQM

EFQM Excellence Model

ENABLERS – CONTRIBUTORY FACTORS TO INCLUSION

1. LEADERSHIP

- Develop aims, objectives, mission, vision and values of inclusion.
- Develop, implement and improve management system for inclusion.
- Ensure school stakeholders and external partners are involved in developing and supporting inclusion activities.
- Ensure school's stakeholders are motivated, encouraged, supported, listened to and recognised for their individual and team efforts in relation to improving inclusive practice.

2. POLICY AND STRATEGY

- Implementing a clear strategy supported by an inclusion policy and action plan.
- Inclusion policy/strategy based on present and future needs/ expectations of stakeholders, in responding to national and local demands.
- Inclusion policy/strategy is based on pupil attainment/progress, quality of teaching and learning, stakeholders' opinions/ideas and the context of the school's intake.
- Inclusion policy/strategy is developed, reviewed and updated, in line with the LEA's inclusion policy and strategy.
- Inclusion policy and strategy is supported by key processes, e.g. identifying inclusion activities, establishing ownership, reviewing the effectiveness of delivery.
- Inclusion policy/strategy is communicated to all within the school, as well as outside in the community.

3. PEOPLE

- Human resources are planned, managed, improved and deployed effectively to support educational inclusion.
- Staff knowledge, competencies on inclusion are identified, developed and sustained through team building and CPD.
- Participants are involved and empowered in the process of improving barrier-free learning and participation for all pupils.
- School management and participants share best practice and communicate regularly about inclusion issues.
- Participants are supported, rewarded and recognised for their contributions to improving educational inclusion.

4. PARTNERSHIPS AND RESOURCES

- External partners are identified who will give value added to improving inclusive practice, share knowledge/expertise and innovate.
- Securing value for money and evaluating expenditure and commitment to improving school's inclusion practices.
- Managing the safe, efficient, effective use of buildings, facilities, equipment, resources to improve inclusive provision for pupils.
- Making the most of existing and new technology to support improvement in educational inclusion.
- Collecting, structuring, generating and managing information and knowledge to support the school's inclusion policy and strategy.

5. PROCESSES

- Systematic design and management of processes related to improving the quality of teaching and barrier-free learning opportunities.
- Improved inclusion processes through the use of innovation and change which satisfy stakeholders, and which act upon their opinions. Maximising on internal and external expertise in order to develop and improve the range of out-of-hours learning activities to support inclusion, as well as to promote barrier-free learning and participation for all pupils. Ongoing staff training supports inclusion.
- Inclusion is based on addressing the needs and expectations of pupils and parents in the present and future.
- Introducing new approaches to inclusive teaching and learning in the school, and communicating and marketing these to current and future school clients, e.g. new curriculum courses, new multimedia learning approaches, new out-of-hours learning activities.
- Enhancing and managing parent/school and pupil/school relationships – responding promptly to any concerns or issues raised in relation to inclusive practice. Involving parents and pupils in any decision-making, and auditing customer satisfaction annually.

RESULTS (OUTCOMES) OF ENHANCING INCLUSIONS

6. CUSTOMER RESULTS

Pupils' and parents' satisfaction/opinions

Perception measures

Evidence from pupil/parent surveys, focus groups, school council, complaints, positive comments.

Satisfaction with inclusive ethos of school; quality of teaching and learning, LSA satisfaction, loyalty of families to the school; willingness of community partners to support the school.

Performance indicators

Positive media coverage of school's inclusion activities/initiatives.

National and local awards obtained, e.g. Investors in People, Quality Mark.

School providing extra and additional inclusion opportunities in comparison with other similar schools.

Improved pupil attainment and achievements.

Better pupil retention rates at school.

7. PEOPLE RESULTS

Staff motivation, satisfaction/opinions

Perception measures

Evidence from surveys, focus groups, interviews, Performance Management Assessments, staff empowerment and career development opportunities; job satisfaction, leadership, management of change, feeling valued, rewards for efforts and inclusion activities/initiatives developed and involved in.

Performance indicators

Staff more competent in inclusive classroom practice.

Training of staff has improved barrier-free learning and participation for pupils.

Increased staff motivation to participate in inclusion activities.

Decrease in staff absenteeism and staff turnover.

Improved opportunities to communicate with others and work collaboratively.

8. SOCIETY RESULTS

Local community satisfaction/opinions

Perception measures

Evidence from surveys, audits, reports, public meetings, LEA, OFSTED inspections.

Increase in positive LEA/school relationships.

School standing/impact improved in local community.

Increased equal opportunities for all.

Increased support for lifelong learning and reduced juvenile crime in neighbourhood.

Performance indicators

Recognition for school by receipt of local and national awards for inclusion, e.g. Beacon status, teaching awards.

More local community partners wishing to become involved in inclusion initiatives with the school.

Good positive OFSTED inspection report.

Local/national media coverage of school's inclusive practice, e.g. web site, video.

9. KEY PERFORMANCE RESULTS
Outcomes and indicators

Performance outcomes

Financial evidence of value for money in improving inclusive practice within the school.

Good attendance figures, oversubscribed school, improved pupil behaviour/attitudes to learning, few if any pupil exclusions, increased pupil attainment, increased take-up for out-of-hours learning activities, and strong climate/culture of success and achievement.

Performance indicators

Significant improvement in quality of teaching and learning.

More staff prepared to share best practice with others, inside and external to the school.

External partnerships have enhanced inclusive practice and contributed to raising standards, particularly among underachieving/potentially underachieving groups of pupils.

(EFQM 1999 & Lloyds TSB 2001: 6–28)

Note: Performance indicators should include all school internal measures for criteria 6 to 9

OFSTED views school self-evaluation as the key to improvement and raising standards, especially when all staff are committed to appraising their own practice critically. Whatever schools think about OFSTED inspections, the framework for inspection provides a valuable means for evaluating educational inclusion against common criteria.

In relation to exploring inclusion in schools, the OFSTED model of school self-evaluation is based upon finding the answers to four initial key questions:

1. How good is our school at being inclusive? (Standards achieved by the full diversity of pupils and their attitudes and behaviour.)
2. What are the school's strengths and weaknesses in relation to inclusion? (Diagnosis, appraisal and evaluation of the work of the school, and how the school is addressing under-achievement among particular groups of pupils.)
3. What must we do as a school to improve our inclusive practice? (How does the school use and act upon its evaluation findings to improve inclusive practice and raise standards?)
4. Has the school got what it takes to move inclusive culture, policy and practice forward? (Strong, visionary, high quality leadership and management, with a united and committed staff.)

OFSTED testing inclusivity in schools

- Are all pupils achieving as much as they can, and deriving the maximum benefit from what the school provides, according to their individual needs?

- Which pupils/groups may not be achieving as much as they can? Why not?

- How aware is the school of these differences? If not, why not?

- How are differences between groups of pupils explained in terms of achievement, teaching and learning and access to curricular opportunities?

- What action has the school taken to raise the standards of attainment of under-achieving pupils? If none, why?

- If action has been taken, is it appropriate and effective?

- What action is being taken by the school to prevent racism and sexism and to prepare pupils for living in a diverse and interdependent society?

(OFSTED 2000: 9)

OFSTED
school self-
evaluation
framework
supporting
inclusion

OFSTED framework to support schools evaluating educational inclusion

CONTEXT AND OVERVIEW

1. **What sort of school is it?**

OUTCOMES

2. **How high are standards?**

2.1. **The school's results and pupils' achievements.**
2.2. **Pupils' attitudes, values and personal development.**

QUALITY OF PROVISION

3. **How well are pupils taught?**
4. **How good are curricular and other opportunities offered to pupils?**
5. **How well does the school care for its pupils?**
6. **How well does the school work in partnership with parents?**

EFFICIENCY AND EFFECTIVENESS OF MANAGEMENT

7. **How well is the school led and managed?**

ISSUES FOR THE SCHOOL

8. **What should the school do to improve further?**

(Ofsted 1999: 1:6)

1. What sort of school is it?

- What is the diversity of pupils in the school?
- How good are working relations across the school?
- Are admissions procedures inclusive?
- Have there been significant key appointments of staff or head teacher to support inclusion?
- Does the school experience pupil or staff transience?
- Does the school improvement plan prioritise educational inclusion?
- Does the school provide good value for money for inclusion?
- What are the school's strengths and weaknesses in relation to inclusion?

2. How high are standards?

2.1. The school's results and pupil's achievements

- How high are standards at the end of each key stage in comparison with national averages and with similar schools?
- Are there variations in achievement among different groups of pupils, and in different subjects?
- Have there been any noticeable trends in the school's results over time?
- Are teacher assessments broadly in line with the National Curriculum tests, or are there major discrepancies?
- Are pupils achieving as high as they could in relation to their prior attainment?
- Does the school analyse the comparative attainment of different groups of pupils?
- How does the school make use of this analysis of information in order to improve barrier-free learning opportunities for any underachieving groups of pupils?

2.2. Pupils' attitudes, values and personal development

- Are there any groups of pupils who find it difficult to engage with school work?
- How do pupils behave in lessons and around school, and relate to each other?
- Are there any groups of pupils over-represented in relation to exclusions, absence or lateness?
- Are there significant variations between different groups in terms of behaviour, attitudes to learning, personal development or school experience?
- Are any pupils experiencing bullying, racial or sexual harassment?
- Are any pupils being treated unfairly, and if so, how and why?

- Are there any pupils who do not form constructive relationships with teachers, support staff or other pupils?
- How far do pupils reflect upon and understand the impact of
  what they do has on others?
- What has the school done to redress pupils' negative, anti-
  school attitudes?
- How far is the inappropriate behaviour of some pupils
  hindering the progress of other pupils' learning, as well as that
  of their own?
- Do pupils take responsibility willingly and demonstrate
  initiative?
- Are pupils tolerant of each other's differences, cultures and
  diversity?

3. How well are pupils taught?

- Is the teaching across the curriculum effective in meeting a
  diversity of pupils' needs?
- What is the impact of teaching on pupils' learning?
- Are lesson objectives shared with pupils?
- Does lesson planning account for pupils' diversity?
- Are AEN pupils' IEPs being implemented, and are they linked
  to teacher planning?
- Do pupils make sufficient progress?
- Are subject teachers secure in their subject knowledge?
- Does the teaching inspire and challenge pupils to understand
  and deepen their knowledge?
- Do pupils understand what they are doing, know how well they
  have done and know how they can improve?
- Are a range of appropriate teaching strategies used?
- Does teaching challenge stereotypes and respect cultural
  diversity?
- Does homework reinforce and/or extend pupils' learning?
- Does assessment of pupils' work guide pupils towards
  improvement?
- Are additional classroom resources such as ICT or support
  staff effectively deployed?
- Are support staff (LSAs) included in teacher planning, and is
  their role explicit?
- Do LSAs mirror the inclusive approaches of teachers in their
  support role?
- Is pupil behaviour management sound, in order to enable them
  to be productive, remain focused and on task, and work at a
  good pace in the inclusive classroom?

4. How good are curricular and other opportunities offered to pupils?

- How good are the curricular and extra-curricular opportunities offered to a diversity of pupils?
- How is the school implementing the National Curriculum inclusion requirements consistently across the curriculum?
- Is the curriculum fully inclusive by ensuring equality of access and opportunity for a diversity of pupils?
- Does the school teach pupils to appreciate and value cultural diversity?
- Does withdrawal teaching reduce pupils' access to a broad and balanced curriculum?
- Do ability sets/groupings lead to negative labelling, segregation, discrimination, prejudice or stereotyping?
- Are there opportunities for a diversity of pupils to attend lunchtime and after-school homework clubs, out-of-hours learning activities?
- Do the school's community links contribute to pupil's learning?
- Does the school have constructive cross-phase links with its feeder schools and colleges?
- Are appropriate vocational and work-related courses provided for 14–19-year-olds?
- Does the school encourage pupils to take responsibility, show initiative and understand about living in a community?
- Does the school help pupils to discriminate between the principles of right and wrong?
- Does the school provide an effective PSHE and Citizenship programme?
- Does the school provide a daily act of collective worship, which helps pupils acquire spiritual awareness and self-knowledge?

5. How well does the school care for its pupils?

- Does the school induct new pupils effectively?
- Does the school provide translators to assist with communication of pupils/parents?
- Does the school support effectively children looked after by the LEA, sick children, young carers, children 'at risk', and those in families under stress?
- Does the school promote good attendance and behaviour?
- Does the school use rewards and sanctions effectively?
- Does the school monitor and assess the impact of strategies for improving behaviour and attendance?
- Does the school deal with bullying and harassment issues promptly and effectively?
- Is the school receptive to dual registration pupils?
- Does the school assess effectively the full diversity of pupils' attainments and progress?

- Does the school use assessment information to inform and guide planning for inclusion?
- Does the school track pupil progress and take appropriate action to raise the attainment of underachieving groups?
- Do pupils have opportunities to assess and evaluate their own performance?
- Does the school ensure the health, safety, care and protection of all pupils?

6. How well does the school work in partnership with parents?

- How do parents view the school in relation to inclusion?
- Are the school's links with parents effective?
- What is the impact of the parents' involvement with the school's inclusion work?
- Are parents satisfied with what the school provides and achieves?
- Do parents receive good quality information, particularly in relation to pupil progress and attainment?
- Are school reports explicit about what pupils need to do to improve, and how parents can help?
- Are parental links, home-school agreements inclusive and supportive of pupils' learning?
- How well does the school help parents to understand what is taught?
- Is information to parents available in a variety of forms and translations?
- Does the school find ways to attract reluctant parents to approach the school?
- Have any national or local initiatives involved parents in promoting good attendance and behaviour of pupils at the school?
- Does the school consult parents about major spending decisions that impact on educational inclusion?
- How well does the school communicate with parents who have disabilities, learning difficulties or live a distance from the school?

7. How well is the school led and managed?

- How do the head teacher, SMT and governing body promote educational inclusion?
- Do the head teacher and the SMT lead by example, establishing good inclusive role models for staff and pupils?
- Do the inclusion strategies taken secure improvement for all pupils?
- How does the school ensure pupils achieve their optimum potential academically and personally?
- Are all key policies across the school committed to inclusion?

- Do key staff linked to inclusion have planned involvement in curriculum development?
- Do subject leaders/coordinators know what needs to be improved in order to make inclusive provision better in their curriculum area?
- Have the appropriate inclusion priorities been identified and are challenging targets set to raise standards, which lead to continual improvement?
- Are school resources and specific grants deployed efficiently and fairly to improve inclusive practice?
- Is effective use made of external expertise, in order to improve the quality of educational inclusion within the school?

8. What should the school do to improve further?

- How effective is the school in relation to being educationally inclusive?
- How well do the different groups of pupils achieve?
- How effective has the teaching been in supporting and improving inclusive provision and the quality of barrier-free learning?
- How effective is the leadership and management of educational inclusion within the school?
- How far has the school become more inclusive since the last OFSTED inspection?
- Has sufficient value added been demonstrated year-on-year, in relation to improvement in pupil attainment?
- Are staff attitudes positive about inclusion, and are teachers' expectations high enough?
- What does the school need to do in order to address any weaknesses in educational inclusion?

(OFSTED 2000)

Quick reference to managing inclusion

Accept everyone can improve
Ensure raising standards is at the core of all planning
Measure standards
Compare own school with other similar schools
Observe teaching to agreed consistent criteria
Evaluate the impact teaching has on learning
Be open when feeding back after lesson observations
Reflect, discuss and consult with other colleagues
Set targets for improvement
Ensure action is supported, monitored and reviewed regularly
Never stop evaluating

(OFSTED 1999: 156)

Reviewing inclusion

	Inclusive culture	Inclusion policy	Curriculum opportunities	Barrier-free teaching and learning	Staff development	Parent partnership
Where are we now?						
Where do we want to go?						
How will we get there?						
What do we have to do?						

Part 4

External partnerships and innovation to support inclusion

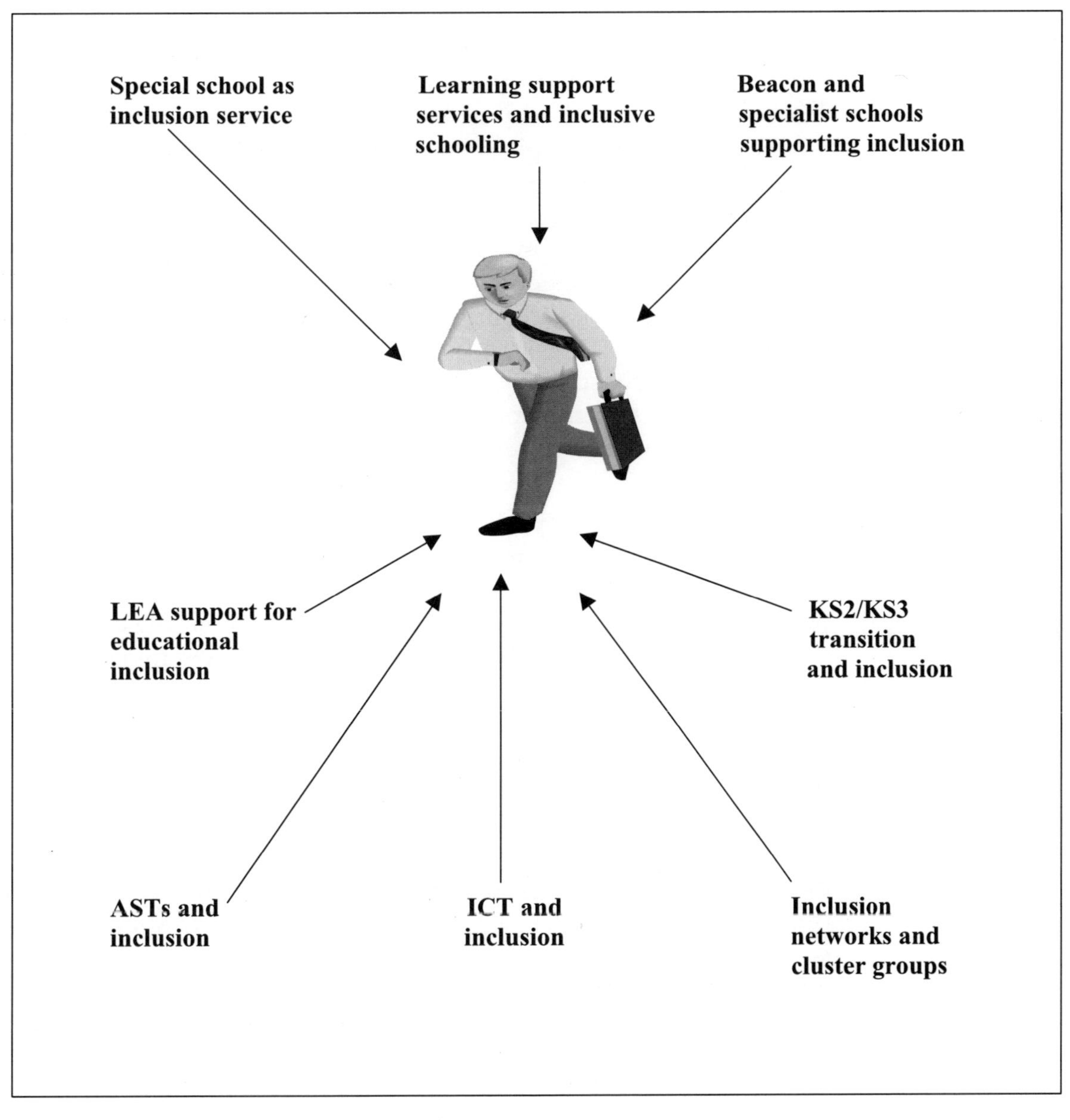

The DfES in recent legislation has continued to emphasise the importance of special schools linking and working closely with mainstream schools, in order to support the development of inclusion.

> Inclusion is about engendering a sense of community and belonging and encouraging mainstream and special schools and others to come together to support each other and pupils with special educational needs. (DfES 2001c: 8)

There is a recognition that the special schools' own pupil population is becoming more complex and wider ranging, and that, in view of this fact, the special school role needs to be redefined. Their changing role can be summarised as follows:

- to become outward-looking centres of excellence;
- to build upon their strengths to form an integral part of an inclusive education system;
- to enable special and mainstream school staff to work more closely together in planning support for SEN children;
- to foster more flexible working arrangements taking some pupils for short-term placements, including other pupils on a longer-term basis in mainstream settings and offering dual registration placements;
- to provide specialist support to SEN children in mainstream placements;
- to act in a consultancy, advisory capacity;
- to provide training and resources to mainstream schools;
- to help mainstream schools to implement inclusion policies.

Both mainstream and special schools need to indicate in their SEN policies the links they are making with each other, to promote inclusion. Some LEAs are refocusing the role of their special school provision by co-locating a special school on the same site as a mainstream school of the same educational phase. Special schools indicate in their inclusion action plans, how they are developing more inclusive links with their mainstream counterparts.

Each special school appoints an Inclusion Coordinator from within their existing staff, who leads a small inclusion team, comprising a teacher and one or two LSAs or nursery nurses. This team facilitates the inclusion of special school children into a range of mainstream placements, for short, medium or long-term periods. It can also offer provision within a specialist classroom setting. When a special school is experiencing falling rolls and surplus places, this new way of working can enhance the professional development of special school staff.

Co-located special school provision can offer an extensive range of inclusion services throughout the borough, which complements the work of the LEA. For example, in one LEA, special schools offered:

- support with the identification of more complex mainstream SEN pupils, by providing short-term assessment placements;
- additional support and advice during SEN pupil transition, between Key Stage (KS) 2 and KS3;
- guidance on enhancing curriculum access in mainstream;
- support to mainstream teachers with the moderation and standardisation of pupils' work, using the 'P' levels;
- support and training to parents/carers of SEN pupils;
- email and videoconferencing facilities between pupils and staff in special and mainstream schools, prior to co-location;
- training, advice and consultancy to early years private, voluntary and independent providers on aspects of SEN identification, policy and provision;
- partnership involvement in a mainstream secondary school's proposed bid for specialist sports college status;
- opportunities for mainstream and special school teachers, LSAs/TAs and nursery nurses to undertake secondments, and 'job-swapping' between settings;
- action research to review and evaluate inclusion projects and initiatives taking place on a local basis.

The continuing existence of special schools is based on the understanding that there will be mutually beneficial learning links with mainstream schools. The way forward is a joint focus on curriculum development.

The Government is explicit in its expectations that special schools will become a complementary and compensatory resource to mainstream schools. Cross-site and cross-curriculum practice will be a priority.

The special school of the future will become part of the mainstream education system, while providing an inclusion service at the same time. Schools need to resolve the dilemmas created by responding to diversity within the framework of a common educational system.

Learning support services and inclusive schooling

Learning support services continue to play a key role in contributing to statutory assessment procedures, and providing direct support to statemented children in mainstream schools, despite increased delegation of funding to schools for these services. Delegated funding responsibility and inclusion are closely linked, and need to occur gradually.

Strategically, delegation of learning support service funding is designed to encourage mainstream schools to take greater ownership and responsibility for fostering inclusive schooling. It also endeavours to change the view that learning support services are merely 'custodians of entitlement' or 'agents of dependence'.

Irrespective of whether mainstream schools recruit and employ their own learning support staff, or 'buy back' the existing learning support service personnel, LEAs and schools have a duty to ensure quality learning support staff are well managed, and receive appropriate ongoing professional development. In addition, schools and LEAs are accountable for ensuring that such provision for supporting pupils learning is closely linked to raising standards.

The National Association for Special Educational Needs (NASEN) undertook a review of the role of LEA SEN support services in England (NASEN 2001). They made the following recommendations regarding developing support for more inclusive schooling.

- Schools should be more open about how much funding they receive for SEN and indicate in their school improvement plan how it is to be used to raise the attainment of pupils with learning difficulties.
- Schools should show evidence of the progression made towards inclusion, and indicate future developments.
- Schools should recognise the changing role of delegated learning support services, and adjust their expectations accordingly, in relation to provision.
- Support services need to set targets to indicate how they will contribute to inclusion developments locally.
- The impact of provision and intervention from delegated learning support services must be monitored and evaluated by LEA officers for best value reviews and value added, particularly in relation to pupil progress.
- LEAs should ensure that schools and services are very clear about each other's roles and responsibilities for providing additional support for learning.

LEAs can monitor and evaluate the work of inclusion consultants and advisory teachers, and core LSAs via observation, and outcomes from service delivery, e.g. client satisfaction (pupils, parents and senior managers in schools), and pupil progress. They can also review how schools are managing delegated staff.

The LEAs' response to the NASEN recommendations

- The LEA may rename the delegated learning support service the Inclusion Advisory Team (IAT).

- IAT will have a strategic manager, who leads a core team of five or six Inclusion Advisory Teachers, allocated on a district basis to clusters of schools.

- The Inclusion Advisory Teachers will provide training to clusters of schools or individual settings, within their district. They will also assist with the identification and assessment of SEN, advise on the provision of specialised programmes and offer practical classroom strategies.

- According to the number of SEN pupils on each school's SEN register at Action Plus and above, existing teachers and LSAs from the service will be delegated to schools who want to 'buy back' their expertise. They will deliver specialist programmes to individual or small groups of pupils, or provide in-class support to enhance curriculum access.

- Senior Inclusion Consultants will support senior managers in using aspects of the Index for Inclusion to support school self-review and school improvement plan inclusion priorities. They will also monitor the impact of delegated service involvement, as well as their own service delivery, in relation to training, advice and consultation.

- Annual analysis of pupil performance data, captured by the LEA, as well as nationally, through schools OFSTED PANDA/PICSIs will provide value added evidence of the progress made by a diversity of pupils receiving additional support, and highlight those who may continue to underachieve.

- A thorough examination of contextual data, such as the level, nature and frequency of additional support offered to pupils in schools, will also be explored. This will help to identify where staff in schools and services who are delivering additional learning and behaviour support to a diversity of pupils would benefit from further professional development, in a drive to raise the attainment of underachieving groups still further, which also includes potential higher attaining pupils.

- The LEA's inclusion targets will also be reviewed annually, in order to establish if sufficient progress has been made towards meeting these.

The major issue for all schools will be how they are managing and deploying additional staff to support pupils' learning needs effectively, including those from delegated services. Contextual issues such as staff expertise, qualifications, attendance rates, roles and responsibilities, will need to be reviewed annually by senior managers.

Beacon and specialist schools supporting inclusion

Beacon schools and specialist schools both promote inclusive practice through their common aim of raising standards in the quality of teaching and learning for a diversity of pupils of all abilities. They both work collaboratively with partners or clusters of schools; they encourage teachers to work and learn together, and they develop ways of supporting and sharing good practice with other schools.

Innovation and partnership form the basis of their working relationship with other schools and with the wider community. Both schools help to sustain and support school improvement through a process of school self-evaluation within their own institutions, as well as in partner schools. The quality and outcomes of their work are measured by the impact on pupils' learning.

The challenge for beacon and specialist schools, in their continuing drive to raise standards, is to tackle underachievement and extend opportunities for all pupils, while maintaining a clear focus on inclusion.

Beacon schools working in the foundation stage, primary and secondary phases promote inclusive practice through a range of activities. For example they may:

- offer a range of advice on specific curriculum subjects;
- support school leadership and management;
- provide guidance and practical strategies on meeting the needs of gifted and talented pupils, SEN children, EBD pupils;
- suggest approaches for improving working with parents/carers;
- provide workshops, seminars, INSET and organise Beacon Days, which all spotlight aspects of their work.

Specialist schools in the secondary phase focus on one of eight specialisms: technology, language, sports, arts, business and enterprise, engineering, science, mathematics and computing.

Specialist schools foster inclusive practice within their own school and among other secondary schools and the wider community, in their specialist subject by:

- building on previous achievements at Key Stage 2 to ensure continuity and progression at Key Stage 3;
- making effective use of technology to support pupils' learning;
- paying close attention to improving pupils' literacy, numeracy and communication skills;

- encouraging pupils to take greater responsibility for their own work, and evaluating their own progress;
- providing a range of enrichment activities to broaden and deepen pupils' experiences, and to extend gifted and talented pupils in particular;
- implementing a system of focused individual pupil target setting, designed to keep them on track;
- introducing the deliberate teaching of study skills, revision and examination techniques, particularly at Key Stage 4;
- mentoring pupils who fall behind with work, or who need further encouragement to maintain their work focus;
- extending the range of accredited courses available to pupils at Key Stage 4 and post-16;
- building partnerships with business and industry to support pupils' learning;
- encouraging paired working between staff, across specialist subjects within the same school;
- providing showcase events, e.g. Saturday Schools, Activity Days or Weeks, focused on specialist subject projects, or supporting pupils' study skills, revision and examination techniques, and assisting with coursework completion.

Specialist schools emphasise social inclusion in particular, and are clearly focused on maintaining and accelerating pupil achievement.

Although this section focuses on KS2 to KS3 transition, the information and guidance offered can support the inclusion and induction of children and young people entering a school or college, at any point within the academic year.

Dimension B.1.5 of the Index for Inclusion (see page 70) audits the inclusion of new pupils. It provides a very useful set of questions for schools to use, when reviewing how inclusive their policies and procedures are, for inducting and welcoming new pupils.

The Chief HMI of schools in his annual report for 2000/01 noted:

> It is vital for secondary schools to build more effectively and quickly on the achievement of pupils moving from primary schools and hence to raise levels of performance at Key Stage 3.

> Inclusion will be truly successful only if we recognise the achievement and progress of all pupils.   (OFSTED 2002a: Commentary)

Cross-phase transition is about ensuring that pupils make a smooth change from their primary to their secondary school, and that their progress is advanced, rather than hampered by this movement between schools.

Supporting inclusion during Key Stage 2 to Key Stage 3 transition

- Does the school have an induction programme for new pupils?

- Does the induction programme take into account pupil differences in attainment and home language?

- Is information regarding transition conveyed to parents/carers in jargon-free, understandable language?

- Are new pupils paired with more experienced pupils on first entering the school?

- Does the school find out how new pupils have settled in, after a few weeks?

- Is there support for any new pupils who have difficulty remembering the location of particular classrooms or specialist areas in the school?

- Are new pupils clear about who they should contact in school if they are experiencing any difficulties in settling in?

- Do secondary school staff collaborate sufficiently to support transition from the previous/present phase to the next phase of education?

Suggested strategies to make KS2/KS3 transition smoother

- Establish a transition network with focus groups comprising staff from the secondary school and feeder primary schools, and any key external personnel, which target particular aspects of transition, e.g. a senior management group concerned with reviewing and evaluating transition arrangements; a pastoral group who organise and oversee the induction programme, and the transfer of pupil information; and finally, a curriculum group who are responsible for ensuring continuity and progression between phases.

- Secondary schools to host joint Easter Schools/Summer Schools or Saturday Schools with Year 6 teachers, with a focus on specific activities related to preparing for transition, e.g. team building exercises, developing thinking skills.

- Run joint primary school/secondary school summer term projects, go on joint educational visits, or organise cross-phase activity days. Incorporate 'peer buddies' into such events, who will support vulnerable pupils at the start of Year 7.

- Hold parent/carer workshops, social events that provide an opportunity for discussion of cross-phase issues, and give advice through self-help parent groups on how to cope with their child's anxieties.

- Encourage Year 7 teachers and LSAs to visit the feeder primary schools and show a video on aspects of social and academic life in Year 7, which has an accompanying pupil commentary, to allay any initial fears or concerns Year 6 pupils may have about transition.

- Organise curriculum progression meetings between subject coordinators/heads of department in both phases during the summer term, prior to transition, and again in the autumn term of Year 7. This should ensure that Year 7 teachers, particularly in the core National Curriculum subjects, are familiar with what forthcoming Year 7 pupils have already covered, and therefore will avoid too much repetition in pupils' learning.

- Hold cross-phase curriculum moderation meetings twice a year, to standardise pupils' work in the core subjects.

- Arrange collaborative team teaching initiatives between secondary school subject teachers and Year 6 teachers. This could support the delivery of the Bridging Units to enable Level 3 pupils to catch up.

- Provide Year 6 pupils with transition information via inter-school web sites, and pupil-friendly brochures. (An example of a pupil transition brochure is included on the following pages.)

© Rita Cheminais 2002

Moving on to Year 7

Welcome from the head teacher

Moving from primary to secondary school is known as transition. This move from Year 6 to Year 7 can be both exciting and yet a worry to new pupils.

This booklet will help you to prepare, well in advance, for the start of your new Key Stage 3 career at Motley High School.

In the booklet you will find details about:

- your first day at school;
- timetables;
- form tutor role;
- helpful tips to cope with worries;
- what the school expects from you, as a pupil;
- what you can expect from Motley High School;
- who to go to for further advice.

I would ask you to share the information in this booklet with your parents/carers.

I look forward to meeting you in September.

Neil Stevens   (Head teacher)

What will happen on my first day?

- You will meet your form tutor in the school hall.
- The form tutor will take you to your form room.
- During the first morning you will be given a printed timetable, a school journal, a homework timetable, and be allocated a locker.
- After morning break you will complete an activity which tells your form tutor about your interests, strengths, talents, as well as, what you find difficult.
- You will do some team building activities to help you get to know other pupils in your form.
- You will be informed about lunch-time arrangements and view the menu offered for food and drink.
- After lunch you will register, and attend lessons in the afternoon. (There will be staff on duty to help you find your way to classrooms.)

What will I need to bring on my first day?

- A school bag
- A note pad, calculator, watch, pocket dictionary
- A pencil case containing: pens, pencil, ruler, rubber, highlighter, coloured pencils, pencil sharpener
- Dinner money or packed lunch

What will my form tutor do?

- Mark the register each day and collect notes of absence.
- Collect any money or return slips from school letters.
- Check your school journal each week.
- Check you are in full school uniform.
- Ensure all members of the form behave properly.
- Listen to any worries, and answer general questions.
- Give praise and encouragement.
- Help you to solve school problems, in general.
- Cheer you up when you feel unhappy or sad.
- Give daily information about any timetable changes or events taking place.
- Give you responsibilities, e.g. register monitor.
- Help you to make friends with others in the form.
- Keep an eye on your progress in school work.
- Help you develop social skills, and teach PSHE.
- Show respect and trust towards you and others.

Which form will I be in?

You are in **FORM 7P**

Your form tutor is: **Miss Johnson**

What school expects from you

- Arrive each day on time.
- Bring the correct equipment and books.
- Work to the best of your ability.
- Complete class work and homework on time.
- Allow other pupils to get on with their work.
- Follow the school rules and behave sensibly.
- Be helpful, polite, respectful and considerate to others at all times.
- Wear full school uniform with pride.
- Look after the school environment, keeping it litter-free and eco-friendly.

What you can expect from Motley High School

- A safe, secure, barrier-free learning environment.
- The provision of learning support and mentoring.
- The opportunity to extend your learning.
- The chance to show your strengths, gifts and talents.
- Guidance on how to become an independent learner.
- Out-of-hours learning activities and lunch-time clubs.
- The chance to voice your opinions through the school council, about aspects of school life.
- Pastoral and academic guidance from staff and older pupils.
- Mutual respect and trust from all staff and pupils.

Year 6 pupil worries and how to cope

<u>Going out of school for a dental or hospital appointment</u> – bring a note or appointment card, tell your form tutor, sign out at the office.

<u>Forgotten your PE kit</u> – contact home to get someone to bring it in, inform the PE teacher before the lesson, borrow spare kit.

<u>Not completed homework</u> – tell the subject teacher the reason why and ask for an explanation of the task, or seek more help.

<u>Arrive late at school</u> – sign in at the school office and give your reason for lateness.

<u>Your coat has gone missing</u> – check at lost property office that it hasn't been handed in; tell your form tutor.

<u>You need to go to the toilet during a lesson</u> – ask the teacher for permission, and take their 'out of class card' with you.

<u>You don't understand the work in a lesson</u> – tell the teacher, and request extra help.

<u>You have lost your school journal</u> – tell your form tutor, check if it has been handed in at the office, buy another school journal.

<u>A Year 10 pupil is taking money from you</u> – tell your form tutor and the Head of Year 7.

What Year 7 pupils say about transition

Who else can help you at Motley High School?

Assistant head teacher:	Mr Coleman
Head of Year 7:	Mr Bates
Key Stage 3 Coordinator:	Mrs Freeman
Coordinator for Gifted and Talented Pupils:	Mr Temple
Head of Learning Support	Mrs Swann
Year 7 Learning Mentors:	Miss Wade Mr Jordan
Student counsellors:	Sally Gold Dave Stone
School librarian:	Mrs Lloyd

Networks, cluster groups, focus groups and working groups, which are created for the purpose of bringing individuals together to address aspects of improving educational inclusion, must have school improvement at the core of their central purpose, in any collaborative partnership.

School improvement can be defined as:

> A systematic, sustained effort aimed at a change in learning conditions and other related internal conditions in one or more schools, with the ultimate aim of accomplishing educational goals more effectively. (van Velzen *et al.* 1985: 48)

A **network** is a forum for individuals to collaborate for mutual benefit, in order to share information, interests, ideas and concerns about aspects of inclusion, with colleagues in similar roles from their own school and other schools. They provide a mechanism for individuals to enhance their ability to solve problems related to inclusion, by interchanging skills and resources. Networking can occur face-to-face, through telephone or videoconferencing, or via the Internet.

David Blunkett, in a speech he delivered to the Social Market Foundation commented on networking:

> Where schools share good practice, tackle common problems and offer specialist opportunities to pupils at a range of schools, each school can help to enhance performance across an area – creating networks of excellence that go beyond a single school.
>
> (DfEE 2000)

Networks for school senior managers, Inclusion Coordinators and SENCOs, coordinated by a General Adviser or a School Improvement Officer from the LEA, which meet each term, can be very effective in disseminating good practice on inclusion.

A **cluster** is a relatively stable collaborative commitment among a group of schools, which come together for mutual benefit, in order to share resources and decision making, in response to inclusion issues, at a local level. School clusters can enhance skills and information interchange, pool resources to maximise the use of expertise and equipment, share INSET and develop specialisms.

Clusters may be permanent or temporary, formal or informal, geographical, single phase, e.g. primary phase; multi-phase, i.e. a secondary school and its feeder primary schools including special schools. They can also involve representatives from external agencies, whose work is focused on aspects of inclusion.

The optimum size recommended for a cluster group to be effective, is between six and eight schools. Clusters benefit from having a key person to coordinate their work, from within one of the cluster schools.

A cluster focused on Key Stage 2 to Key Stage 3 transition and inclusion, for example, can enable identification of a diversity of pupils who may experience barriers to learning, to be clarified. It can improve continuity and progression in pupils' learning through advanced planning, in relation to the appropriate provision required in the next phase of education, to meet the pupils' learning needs.

A **focus group** comprises 10 or 12 individuals in an LEA or within a school, which may include representatives from pupils, staff, parents, governors, members of the local community, who portray a range of viewpoints. Its function is to gather and provide a large amount of relevant information, in an open and transparent manner, as quickly as possible.

A focus group allows members to discuss inclusion issues, to arrive at consensus where there is agreement, and identify any significant differences of opinion. A school's focus group may take a broad view of educational inclusion as a whole, or it may provide feedback on specific inclusion aspects, related to culture and ethos, policy and practice.

Where an LEA focus group reviews inclusion within the borough, it is able to reach consensus about the concept of inclusion, produce an agreed LEA inclusion policy and a council strategy, which informs school improvement and drives raising standards for all children educated in its local schools.

Working groups in schools can be formed in order to address a particular key issue or priority relating to inclusion on the school improvement plan. The group will have a clear purpose, and comprise a fair representation of school stakeholders, while receiving the interest and support of the senior management team. These groups work informally and can utilise brainstorming, survey and action research techniques, in order to find solutions.

ICT supporting inclusion

ICT in inclusive schools is viewed as an integral part of teaching, learning and managing. It contributes significantly to school improvement, helps to raise standards in teaching and learning, and includes all pupils within the full ability range.

Each National Curriculum subject requires pupils to be taught where and how to use ICT in order to support their learning and achievements in all subjects. Information technology is one of the six key skills, which are to be developed across the curriculum. Pupils are expected to use a range of information sources and ICT tools to find, analyse, interpret, evaluate and present information for a range of purposes, as well as using it for problem solving, decision making and creative activities.

Incorporating ICT into teaching is successful when:

- it helps pupils to meet the learning objectives set;
- pupils have frequent access to appropriate technology;
- it is evident across all curriculum areas;
- pupils are able to transfer and apply ICT skills in a range of learning contexts.

A recent OFSTED report on ICT in schools commented:

> The effectiveness of ICT use in the classroom is often demonstrated by the extent to which it engages pupils and sustains their attention . . . By extending the learning context, ICT often provides increased stimulus.   (OFSTED 2002b: 38)

OFSTED considers that the effective application of ICT across subjects still needs to improve. Monitoring the impact that ICT has on improving teaching and learning is crucial.

ICT supports all learners in an inclusive classroom by:

- including pupils as active participants in classroom activities;
- offering pupils the opportunity to utilise different learning styles;
- motivating pupils to learn and remain focused on task;
- enabling pupils to become independent learners;
- enabling pupils to work at their own pace;
- providing pupils with the opportunity to demonstrate their true ability and potential;
- facilitating social communication and interaction, via email;
- enabling pupils to produce well-presented, high quality work outcomes;
- encouraging pupils to publish for a wider audience.

ICT is a useful tool for teachers because it:

- enables them to differentiate and tailor tasks to match pupils' varying skills and abilities;
- facilitates curriculum continuity and progression;
- provides an interesting means of presenting materials to pupils, which will engage, stimulate and motivate;
- enables them to produce high quality learning materials;
- increases their access to a wider range of teaching and learning resources from the Internet;
- facilitates networking and collaboration between teachers, to share ideas, best practice and resources via web sites and email conferencing;
- supports record keeping in relation to pupil progress.

Teachers need to feel confident and able to teach the use of ICT within the curriculum. In addition, Teaching Assistants and Learning Support Assistants need to be familiar with the use of ICT, in order to enable them to enhance and extend pupils' learning across a range of curriculum areas.

The following examples indicate how ICT can reduce barriers to learning for the full ability range of pupils, throughout all key stages, in the inclusive classroom.

- Interactive whiteboards help to raise pupils' expectations when used to demonstrate learning outcomes.

- Digital cameras can be used imaginatively to construct good visual effects, which can be incorporated into the production of a range of school promotional brochures.
- Email communication can be used by pupils and staff to exchange work in progress, especially in relation to homework activities, however; a careful approach to the use of email is a safety issue that must be closely monitored by schools.
- Three-dimensional computer-aided design (CAD) software can enable pupils to produce high quality examples of design work, which can also incorporate sound effects and music.
- The use of web-based research using the Internet in lessons to set searches and bookmark known sites, is valuable when it incorporates an analytic and evaluative element, and is not simply used for reproducing information.
- Provision of a school cyber café can encourage pupils to extend their ICT skills beyond the constraints of lesson time.
- The use of digital projectors, scanners, multimedia software and desktop publishing packages can enhance and extend pupils' learning outcomes, particularly in subjects such as art and design.
- Pupils and staff can become skilled web authors, and via their school website they can celebrate success, share good practice, and strengthen partnership relationships within the community and between schools.
- School, or LEA web sites can support the moderation and assessment of pupils' work, by illustrating on the site, exemplar materials that match the 'P' level and National Curriculum level descriptors.
- Computer-assisted learning (CAL) programmes, such as 'Success Maker', can be used by pupils independently, to improve their basic skills, and provide opportunities for further practice and reinforcement.

ICT can be used as a tool for demonstration, exposition or instruction, which contributes to improvements in pupils' learning. In particular, when pupils use computers in the classroom, they feel in control of their own learning, and are more likely to feel confident about taking risks in learning. Computers are equitable and non-judgemental about their users, and therefore promote educational inclusion for all children and young people.

A visionary LEA, committed to innovation and working in partnership with its schools, will actively promote increased educational inclusion to ensure achievement and progress for all children and young people, through its Education Development Plan priorities and activities.

All schools will be encouraged to use the Index for Inclusion as part of the school self-evaluation process, in order to identify existing strengths as well as areas for further development, in relation to

LEA support for educational inclusion

educational inclusion. Following the audit, an inclusion action plan will be devised and incorporated within the school improvement plan.

The General Adviser for SEN and Inclusion and/or the Team Leader for Inclusion and Diversity within the LEA, along with the Inclusion Consultants or Advisory Teachers, will take the lead responsibility in supporting schools in this process. In addition, they will evaluate and monitor the impact of the effectiveness of the inclusion action plan, as well as any additional support and training provided to the school on inclusion and enhancing barrier-free learning and participation.

In order to establish a consistent approach across the authority, the suggested model below could be implemented, on an annual basis.

Stage 1

Criteria for providing additional support to schools for inclusion are made explicit, and are based on one or more of the following factors:

- low pupil attainment (E, E* PANDA grades);
- minimal value added;
- underachieving cohorts of pupils (EBSD, EAL, SEN, gifted and talented, girls/boys);
- SEN/Inclusion a key issue arising from a school's recent OFSTED inspection report;
- categorisation of schools – special measures, serious weaknesses, underachieving, causing concern, and school self-referral or nomination.

Stage 2

Initial meeting with the head teacher, and an audit of inclusion undertaken in the school.

Stage 3

A contract is drawn up for the provision of additional support and intervention from the Inclusion Consultants/Advisory Teacher, which outlines the partnership agreement.

Stage 4

The level and nature of additional funding and support, the expectations in relation to monitoring and evaluating the impact of LEA intervention are clarified.

Stage 5

Support is provided for the production of the school's inclusion action plan.

Stage 6

The school's inclusion action plan is monitored and reviewed. The effectivness of additional support and funding, consultancy and any training provided is evaluated.

Stage 7

The General Adviser for SEN/Inclusion and the Inclusion Consultants/Advisory Teachers for Inclusion meet to discuss which schools no longer require targeted intervention, and which schools still need to continue being supported.

Advanced skills teachers supporting inclusion

Advanced skills teachers (ASTs) act as a link with the LEA in implementing strategies for promoting educational inclusion. They play a key role in raising the standards of teaching and learning in primary and secondary schools. ASTs contribute considerable expertise to supporting the professional development of trainee teachers, newly qualified teachers (NQTs) and established teachers, within their own schools, and in other schools, working in an outreach capacity. The AST spends 20 per cent of their time (equivalent to one day per week) working with other teachers.

An AST is externally assessed as being an excellent teacher, and someone who achieves the very highest standards of classroom practice. They have:

- high level skills in teaching, classroom management and maintaining discipline;
- high quality planning, assessment and evaluation;
- excellent command of subject knowledge;
- excellent understanding of a diversity of pupils' needs;
- high expectations of themselves and of their pupils;
- the ability to give high quality advice and support to other teachers.

The features listed above are essential in the dissemination and sharing of best inclusive practice, with other teachers, related to improving barrier-free learning opportunities for all.

When ASTs work within their own schools, they are likely to undertake the following activities to promote inclusive practice.

- Provide model demonstration lessons.
- Show how to match teaching approaches to pupils' preferred learning styles.
- Support other colleagues in improving classroom management and organisation.
- Support the production of high quality differentiated teaching materials, which may incorporate the use of multimedia or ICT.
- Develop curriculum resource packs.
- Coordinate the assessment and analysis of pupils' progress, e.g. through supporting the moderation and standardisation of pupils' work.
- Provide practical strategies aimed at reducing underachievement among particular cohorts of pupils, e.g. EAL, disaffected boys, gifted and talented children.
- Update existing schemes of work and support their introduction.
- Participate in the delivery of INSET, focused on raising standards in teaching and learning.
- Provide a structured programme of advice and support and act as a positive role model to teachers experiencing difficulties.
- Mentor trainee teachers and NQTs, and oversee their personal action plans.
- Contribute to the assessment of students on teaching practice.

Within their outreach role, ASTs work with teachers in other schools, categorised as having serious weaknesses, in special measures, underachieving or causing concern. In these instances an LEA adviser will coordinate the work of ASTs to ensure they support the priorities in the LEA Education Development Plan (EDP), focused on raising standards in schools and improving inclusive practice. Their work is likely to cover the following aspects:

- providing direct support to teachers working in schools in challenging circumstances;
- providing exemplar lessons, observed by teachers from a cluster of schools in an area;
- participating in the LEA NQT Induction programme;
- participating in LEA INSET, focused on improving teaching and learning and disseminating best practice.

Outreach work is important for ASTs because it helps them to further develop their own continuing professional development, by providing them with broader experiences and new challenges. It is also essential that ASTs have the opportunity to network with others in similar posts elsewhere, either on a local or regional basis. Email conferencing or web site forums for ASTs provide a useful communication network for exchanging ideas, seeking advice, and sharing information and best practice.

Schools receiving inputs from an AST, as self-evaluating organisations, need to review the impact that they have had on improving
the quality of teaching, raising pupil attainment and enhancing
inclusive practice.

Appendix 1

Barriers to learning – Teacher identification checklist

(Place a tick by the barriers to learning you consider the named pupil to experience in your subject)

Pupil name: _______________________________ **Class/Form:** __________

- ☐ Pupil's preferred learning style does not enable them to understand the subject fully
- ☐ An additional educational need inhibits subject access
- ☐ Difficult to engage in the learning process
- ☐ Easily distracted by other peers, during lessons
- ☐ Poor organisational skills in evidence
- ☐ Pupil's own emotional, behavioural and social development impairs their own learning
- ☐ Difficulty concentrating and remaining on task
- ☐ Pupil appears to be misplaced in this subject set/group
- ☐ Attendance at lessons is erratic
- ☐ Limited amounts of written work are produced each lesson
- ☐ Reluctance, fear to demonstrate knowledge, gifts and talents in front of other peers
- ☐ Tasks set are not completed in allocated time
- ☐ Instructions have to be repeated and explained more than once
- ☐ Reluctance to accept a higher level of challenge – underachieving
- ☐ Lack of understanding in relation to subject specific/technical vocabulary
- ☐ Homework is often incomplete or handed in late
- ☐ Unable to work cooperatively with other peers in lessons
- ☐ Reluctant to seek help from teacher or LSA in lesson
- ☐ Will not accept that they experience difficulties in learning
- ☐ Lacks motivation and shows little interest in the subject

Teacher signature: _______________________________ Date: __________

Subject: ____

Please return this checklist to the Inclusion Coordinator.

© Rita Cheminais 2002

Appendix 2

Pupil inclusion survey

Year group: _________ **Class:** _________________   **Male** ☐   **Female** ☐

Put a tick in **one** box for your answer to each question.

QUESTIONS	YES	SOMETIMES	NO
1. The school is welcoming and inclusive	☐	☐	☐
2. I feel safe in school	☐	☐	☐
3. The school is clean and tidy	☐	☐	☐
4. Teachers and support staff are friendly and helpful	☐	☐	☐
5. All pupils are treated fairly in school	☐	☐	☐
6. Pupils help each other	☐	☐	☐
7. Pupils treat each other with respect	☐	☐	☐
8. Pupil behaviour in school is good	☐	☐	☐
9. There are a good range of clubs/after-school activities	☐	☐	☐
10. Homework help/study support is available	☐	☐	☐
11. I get bored in lessons	☐	☐	☐
12. Teachers deal with pupils who bully others	☐	☐	☐
13. I can talk to a teacher if I am upset or worried	☐	☐	☐
14. Teachers make lessons fun and interesting	☐	☐	☐
15. I like working with other pupils in lessons	☐	☐	☐
16. Teachers know how I learn best	☐	☐	☐
17. If I find learning hard, teachers help me	☐	☐	☐
18. I am allowed to ask questions and share ideas	☐	☐	☐
19. Teachers listen to me and let me explain my thinking	☐	☐	☐
20. Teachers tell me how I can improve my work	☐	☐	☐
21. I can use the school library in lesson time	☐	☐	☐
22. Computers can be used in lessons	☐	☐	☐

	YES	SOMETIMES	NO
23. I get the right amount of homework	☐	☐	☐
24. It is OK to show others your talents/knowledge	☐	☐	☐
25. I feel valued as a member of the school	☐	☐	☐

List **three** things that would improve the school for pupils.

a) ____

____

____

b) ____

____

____

c) ____

____

____

Thank you for answering all the questions
Post your survey in the red box in the main entrance of school

Appendix 3

Inclusion referral sheet

Name of pupil: ____

Form/Class: ____

Subject pupil experiencing barriers to learning in: _______________________

Teacher making referral: _______________________________________

Current level of performance in subject: _________________________

Potential performance level in subject: _________________________

Sources of evidence on which the referral is made:
(list the main barriers to learning the pupil is frequently experiencing in the subject)

Additional evidence to indicate that the pupil is under-performing:
(e.g. test results, samples of homework/class work attached)

Recommended strategies and additional resources to remove barriers to learning:

Targets to enable pupil to reach optimum potential:

1. ____

2. ____

3. ____

Teacher signature: ___________________________ **Date:** _________

Pupil signature: _____________________________ **Date:** _________

© Rita Cheminais 2002

WANTED

Study buddies

**Can you spare some time
every week to give a
younger pupil study
support?**

Interested?

Want to find out more?

**Contact Mr Fraser in the OASIS Centre
and ask for an application form**

© Rita Cheminais 2002

Certificate
of
Study Support

This is to certify that

____

has completed training and offered study support to younger pupils at High Hills School for one year

The skills acquired were:

- problem solving
- decision-making
- study techniques
- learning styles
- confidence building
- listening skills

Head teacher ___________________________

Inclusion Coordinator ___________________________

Date ___________________________

© Rita Cheminais 2002

Example of a subject inclusion policy

Introduction

This is an open, accessible policy that supports inclusive education in science. Every pupil has an entitlement to reach their full potential in science, within a barrier-free learning environment. Science is a collaborative subject, which by its very nature fosters cooperative learning and risk taking.

Aims and objectives

The science inclusion policy will:

- minimise barriers to learning and participation;
- provide a range of appropriate teaching and learning approaches to match pupils' individual needs;
- provide equality of educational opportunity for all pupils;
- ensure that the policy is implemented consistently by all staff teaching science;
- ensure that all pupils have access to an appropriately differentiated science curriculum;
- ensure that appropriate assessment procedures are used in science, which recognise the progress of pupils with additional educational needs (AEN).

Coordinating inclusive provision in science

The subject leader/head of department is responsible for implementing, monitoring and evaluating the effectiveness of the inclusion science policy throughout all key stages, within the school. All teachers of science are responsible for ensuring that all pupils receive their entitlement to barrier-free learning opportunities.

The department has a nominated inclusion representative for the subject, who is responsible for liaising with the school's Inclusion Coordinator. The science inclusion representative's role is to:

- assist in identifying pupils experiencing barriers to learning in science;
- advise on appropriate subject specific resources and schemes of work that will reduce barriers to learning and participation in science for pupils with AEN;

- disseminate best inclusive practice in science, among other colleagues within the department;
- attend relevant inclusion team meetings.

A range of identification strategies will be used which include:

- records of pupils' progress in relation to science curriculum level descriptors
- teacher assessment
- samples of pupils' work
- evidence from lesson observations
- evidence of barriers to learning as recorded on generic checklist
- pupil self-identification
- parents' and carers' concerns

Identification of barriers to learning and participation in science

In line with the statutory National Curriculum inclusion statement, all teachers of science will:

- set suitable learning challenges in the subject, which enable pupils to experience success and make progress;
- respond to pupils' diverse learning needs by raising expectations, securing pupil motivation and concentration, using appropriate teaching and assessment approaches and setting suitable challenging learning targets;
- overcome potential barriers to learning and assessment for pupils by using appropriate curriculum resources, ICT, creating a supportive learning environment in science lessons, setting realistic demands and providing positive feedback to pupils on their learning.

Inclusive provision in science

The science department offers a continuum of provision to meet a diversity of pupils' additional educational needs. Pupils are taught in mixed ability groups in Years 7 and 8, and in-class support is available from LSAs, for pupils identified as experiencing barriers to learning. Some pupils may also benefit from short-term intervention in the school's OASIS Centre in order to further develop and improve pupils' generic skills in thinking, problem solving and study techniques. Pupils in Year 9 are taught in ability sets, but there are opportunities for pupils to move between sets, according to their rate of progress. In Key Stage 4, pupils follow appropriate courses, which lead to recognised qualifications in science. All pupils obtain a science qualification, which matches their level of ability. Some pupils in Years 10 and 11 will benefit from support from LSAs and access to the facilities offered by the OASIS Centre, in relation to completing coursework and developing revision techniques. ICT is available in all science classrooms, with Internet access. The OASIS Centre can provide pupils with opportunities to use other multimedia facilities, as alternative methods of recording their work outcomes. Subject mentoring, educational science visits, opportunities to enter competitions or be involved in school science projects and to attend the science club are open to all interested pupils.

Resources for inclusion

The subject leader/head of department submits an inclusion resource proposal each January, to the school's Inclusion Coordinator. This identifies the inclusion priorities in science, which also reflect the inclusion objectives in the school improvement plan. The subject leader outlines the additional resources required with approximate costs, and justifies how these will improve inclusive practice within the science department. Resources may include: extra curriculum materials, additional in-class support, or professional development for science teachers.

Inclusive assessment procedures in science

A consistent system of assessing pupils' progress in science is used, which conforms to nationally recognised assessment systems, e.g. 'P' level descriptors, National Curriculum levels, including exceptional performance descriptors for gifted and talented pupils in science. Teachers are provided with a baseline assessment for all pupils in their classes, at the beginning of each academic year in science, in order to ascertain their current level of functioning. Pupils are then reassessed after six months, and again at the end of the academic year, in order to record value added progress. All science teachers moderate and standardise samples of pupils' work in order to ensure that accurate teacher assessments are being made consistently within the department. Parents are kept informed of their child's progress in science through the school's reporting system. Pupils are also encouraged to assess their own progress in the subject.

Evaluating the science inclusion policy

The policy is reviewed at the end of the academic year by the subject leader, in order to establish how far it has been successful in improving barrier-free learning and participation opportunities in science. The evidence of the effectiveness of the science inclusion policy is obtained from pupil attainment data, the impact of inclusion INSET within the department, and by improvements made through access to LSAs and the OASIS Centre.

Model inclusive teaching and learning policy

This policy acts as a point of reference for staff to guide them in providing an effective, well-managed learning environment, in which the individual child can thrive and flourish, and learn through their total experience.

Introduction

This teaching and learning policy has been approved by the staff and governors of the school. Pupils' learning is the core purpose of the school, and their contributions are encouraged and valued. The school believes that all pupils should realise their optimum potential by receiving a wide range of high quality, barrier-free challenging learning experiences and opportunities. Diversity is valued as a rich resource which supports the learning of all children, in a happy, caring, secure learning community, which promotes excellence.

Vision statement

The school aims to:

Aims

- provide pupils with a range of varied learning activities and tasks which are responsive to their different learning styles;
- address pupils' individual learning needs through the use of effective teaching approaches;
- make effective use of a range of well-presented curriculum materials and resources to match pupils' learning interests and aspirations;
- engage pupils fully as active participants in the learning process;
- recognise and address any underachievement through appropriate teaching and learning programmes;
- acknowledge and promote parental involvement and partnership in pupils' learning.

Objectives The school's objectives are to:

- ensure the school's teaching and learning policy is implemented consistently by all staff;
- identify and remove barriers to learning;
- ensure pupils have access to appropriately differentiated curriculum learning opportunities to match their ability;
- ensure the classroom ethos and environment supports learning;
- ensure pupils are clear about the expected learning outcomes;
- ensure lessons are well structured, have a brisk pace and provide opportunities to extend and review learning;
- ensure teachers' planning takes account of continuity and progression in learning, and takes account of pupils' prior attainment;
- ensure teachers know how pupils learn best;
- ensure pupils receive feedback on how they can improve their learning.

Definitions The Campaign for Learning defines learning as:

> . . . a process of active engagement with experience. It is what people do when they want to make sense of the world. It may involve an increase in skills, knowledge, understanding, values and the capacity to reflect. Effective learning leads to change, development and a desire to learn.

Learning entails:

- acquiring more or new knowledge
- memorising and reproducing knowledge
- applying facts or procedures
- understanding
- seeing something in a different way
- change in a person.

Children learn best when they are:

- learning predominantly in their preferred style;
- using both sides of the brain;
- actively involved in the learning process;
- given opportunities to ask questions and express opinions;
- answering open-ended questions;
- taught how to learn;
- given opportunities to regularly review their learning;
- happy, interested, motivated, feeling confident and secure in the learning environment;
- able to achieve success and gain approval;
- clear about what they are expected to do;
- challenged, inspired and stimulated;
- given the opportunity to work individually, in pairs, groups and as a whole class;
- provided with opportunities to discuss their learning.

Teachers create effective learning environments in which stereotypical views are challenged. Pupils learn to view others' differences positively. They experience world culture in their learning. Teaching approaches provide equality of opportunity, as well as maintaining pupil motivation and concentration. The learning culture is child-centred, values pupils' own interests and learning styles. It fosters independent learning and initiative, and is open to others' ideas. The appropriate learning culture utilises a variety of learning resources. It encourages pupils to understand the factors that help them to progress in their learning. Incorrect pupil answers to questions in lessons are utilised as productive opportunities for learning, which encourage creative thinking.

Teaching in this school, is seen as the art of awakening the natural curiosity of young minds.

All teachers observe the National Curriculum inclusion principles of:

- setting suitable learning challenges
- responding to pupils' diverse learning needs
- overcoming barriers to learning and assessment for individuals and groups of pupils

Having a clear understanding about different learning styles enables teachers to set appropriate learning challenges for a diversity of pupils in their lessons.

Effective teaching in this school is characterised by:

- clear planning to meet pupil diversity;
- well-structured lessons, which have an opening, a main part and a plenary;
- lessons being delivered using a variety of teaching approaches;
- a classroom climate based on mutual respect and focused on learning;
- assessment, recording and reporting of pupils' progress that informs planning and teaching;
- clear learning objectives set which are shared with and understood by pupils;
- the teacher modelling and demonstrating expected learning outcomes;
- high expectations;
- good discipline and behaviour management;
- the effective use of resources, which may include IT, Teaching Assistants;
- pupils being encouraged to take greater responsibility for their own learning;
- classroom displays being utilised to extend, support and enhance pupils' learning;
- teachers having secure subject knowledge;
- homework being used to extend, review and consolidate learning.

Roles and respon- sibilities

The deputy head teacher is responsible for monitoring the teaching and learning policy. He/she reports annually to the governing body on the effectiveness of this school policy. The deputy head teacher coordinates cross-phase transition with a particular emphasis being placed on ensuring continuity and progression in pupils' learning occurs.

The head teacher monitors and evaluates the quality of teaching and learning throughout the school, within performance management assessment procedures.

The senior management support the continuing professional development of staff in relation to improving teaching and learning, and addressing any issues arising from pupil underachievement.

Subject coordinators are responsible for overseeing that their subject policy, schemes of work and programmes of study keep teaching and learning as a key focus.

All teachers are responsible for the quality of teaching and learning within their classroom.

The Learning Mentor provides a bridge between home and school, in motivating and supporting any disaffected learners.

Teaching Assistants provide targeted additional learning support, which is delivered within the classroom to extend learning and enhance curriculum access. Alternatively, they may deliver a specific learning programme as part of a 'catch-up' learning scheme, to narrow the learning gap for specific pupils.

Peer mentors who act as 'study buddies' are also utilised to provide positive role models in the learning process, to younger peers throughout the school.

Pupils are also encouraged to take greater responsibility for their own learning, particularly in Key Stage 2.

Provision and resources

The school offers a continuum of teaching and learning provision to meet a diversity of pupils' needs. Although all classes are mixed ability, class teachers have the flexibility to set smaller ability groups, within their class, for more focused learning, particularly in relation to literacy and numeracy.

ICT and multimedia learning resources are available in each classroom to support and extend pupils' learning. The school library and learning resource centre is also available for use during and after lessons.

Every class has access to an additional Teaching Assistant, whose key role is to improve curriculum access, and extend and consolidate pupils' learning during their learning support work.

A range of out-of-hours and extra-curricular learning activities to enhance and extend pupils' learning experiences are available during lunch-time and after school. These include: a craft club, 'ECO' club, homework club, thinking club, computer club, chess club, drama club, school band and choir, various sports activities, and residential adventure activity weekends.

All staff incorporate accelerated learning techniques and thinking skills as component parts of their regular classroom teaching.

All teaching staff are responsible for ensuring that their classroom displays are regularly renewed, and contribute to extending and supporting pupils' learning.

External support and partnerships are also utilised by staff within the school, in order to enrich pupils' learning experiences. Links have been made with local beacon and specialist schools to support learning cross-phase. Participation in literacy, numeracy, and gifted and talented summer and Easter schools is a regular feature for Year 6 pupils. Every year, each class is involved in an activity day, when the whole class focuses on an interactive learning initiative. These activity days are featured on the school's web site. Artists and poets in residence, as well as sports personalities, contribute to the enrichment of pupils' learning experiences, annually.

Assessment

Assessment is an integral part of the teaching and learning process. All children are entitled to have their learning achievements and progression recognised. The school has a policy for assessment, recording and reporting. This policy is consistently followed by all staff.

All teachers observe, assess, reflect and review the achievements of each pupil on a regular basis. All teachers keep detailed assessment records on the pupils they teach. Every pupil is fully involved in the assessment process through self-appraisal and target setting. Pupils know what National Curriculum level of attainment they are operating at, and also what they have to do to reach the next level. Assessment is viewed as an ongoing process, which takes account of pupils' different rates of learning development.

End of unit tests and external examinations are useful forms of summative assessment. The outcomes from these tests, as well as ongoing teacher formative assessment, provide parents/carers with evidence of their child's learning achievements.

Any weaknesses in pupils' learning are identified early, and this helps teachers to evaluate the effectiveness of their teaching at regular intervals.

Pupils are given regular constructive feedback on their learning, and this helps them to know when they have mastered a skill, or how they can improve.

Teachers make ongoing observations of pupils' learning in their lessons. They also regularly analyse pupils' work, in order to identify their learning needs.

Assessment also informs continuity and progression in pupils' learning, as they move from one teacher or class to another.

Pupils' learning achievements are also recognised through teachers' verbal praise, having their work displayed in the classroom, the awarding of points and certificates of achievement, and opportunities to celebrate pupils' learning achievements in school assemblies.

Professional development

The school recognises that training for all staff is crucial to the successful implementation of the teaching and learning policy. The senior management team and governing body support and encourage in-service training for staff, in relation to improving the quality of teaching and learning. Training is provided either in-house, by the LEA advisory team, advanced skills teachers, consultants, or external providers. The purpose of the INSET is to enable staff to appreciate that effective teaching enhances the learning of all children, and extends their teaching repertoire.

It also enables teachers to feel more confident and better equipped to meet a diversity of learning needs in the mixed ability teaching context. In addition, it encourages the staff to take greater responsibility for identifying their own continuing professional development needs.

Parent partnership

The school works very closely with parents and carers in order to help pupils achieve their optimum potential, and overcome any barriers to learning.

The school recognises the importance of a positive partnership with parents/carers.

Parents and carers are viewed as essential partners in the learning process. They have vital knowledge and unique insight into how their child learns best. Activities undertaken beyond the classroom, e.g. homework, rely on the support of parents/carers to ensure success.

Parents/carers are encouraged to attend parents evenings, open evenings, parent workshops. Alternative arrangements can be made regarding telephone contact, or home visits to meet with parents/carers, in order to discuss their child's progress in learning. Any parents/carers who have concerns about their child's learning are invited to make an appointment with the class teacher.

Good open, two-way communication between home and school is essential. Parents/carers also have access to information on how they can support their child's learning at home, via study support leaflets, which are available in alternative versions, e.g. CD, video, audio cassette, school web site, as well as in a variety of languages.

Monitoring the policy

The deputy head teacher annually reviews the teaching and learning policy, as part of the whole-school self-evaluation procedure. The effectiveness of the policy in raising standards in the quality of teaching and learning is evaluated using the following performance indicators.

- analysis of pupil attainment data;
- scrutiny of teacher planning;
- lesson observations;
- sampling of pupils' work from across the curriculum;

- analysis of teachers' marking and comments on pupils' written work;
- tracking individual pupils, or cohorts of pupils;
- sampling of reports to parents on pupil progress;
- discussions with pupils about their progress;
- discussions with teachers about pupil progress;
- evaluations from the impact of staff INSET on teaching and learning;
- evaluation of the impact of additional resources, e.g. Learning Mentors, Teaching Assistants, ICT;
- evidence from parental and pupil surveys/questionnaires;
- evidence from subject audits;
- success in meeting teaching and learning priorities on the school improvement plan;
- reduction in the number of pupils excluded from school, or referred for additional learning support;
- improved continuity and progression in pupils' learning, during cross-phase transition;
- reports from the School Link Adviser/School Improvement Officer;
- evidence from the school's Ofsted inspection report.

Conclusion

The evidence gathered from monitoring the impact of the teaching and learning policy engages all stakeholders in the process. The senior management team present the governing body with the value added evidence on how teaching and learning has improved annually.

Maple Primary School

My Learning Log

This learning log belongs to:

____

In class: _______________________________________

I learn best by:

seeing and looking

hearing and listening

making and doing

When do you find learning easy?

When do you find learning hard?

What stops you learning in class?

When do you enjoy learning most?

**How do you remember what you
have learnt, or revise for a test?**

What would help you to learn better?

How do you like to learn in class?

On your own   ☐

With a friend   ☐

In a group   ☐

With the whole class   ☐

What sort of things do you like to use when you are learning?

Computer ☐   TV/video ☐

Radio ☐   Personal CD/cassette player ☐

Books, e.g. encyclopaedia, dictionary, thesaurus ☐

Where else do you like to learn?

Who helps you to learn?

Teachers	☐	Parents	☐
Teaching Assistant	☐	Brothers/sisters	☐
Learning Mentor	☐	Grandparents	☐
Friends	☐	Aunts/uncles	☐
Study Buddy	☐	Neighbours	☐

How do you know when you have learnt something well?

When do you talk about your learning?

Who has taught you how to learn?

**What is the most important thing
you have learnt?**

**What is the most interesting thing
you have learnt?**

**What is the least useful thing
you have learnt?**

When do you find learning boring?

Do you find homework helps your learning?

**Who do you tell if you have
problems learning?**

What else would you like to learn about?

Appendix 9

How well am I doing in my school work?

Subject: ________________________________ **Date of Review:** ___________

Answer all the questions about your progress in this subject.

1. **What National Curriculum level or 'P' level are you currently working at?**

2. **What level of attainment do you expect to achieve at the end of the school year?**

3. **What do you consider yourself to be good at in this subject, e.g. what are your strengths?**

4. **What aspects of the subject do you think you need to improve in?**

5. **What will you have to do to make the required improvements?**

6. **Is there anything else that would help your learning and improvement in this subject?**

7. **Who will help you to achieve your final attainment outcome?**

8. **How will you judge if you are making the required progress?**

9. **Who will you talk to about your attainment and progress?**

10. **Do you have the chance to assess and compare your work with that of other pupils in this class?**

Listed above are some suggested questions that pupils could use as part of a self-assessment process. They are appropriate for any phase of education. Inclusion must engage pupils as active participants in their own self-assessment of progress.

References and further reading

Blandford, S. (1997) *Middle Management in Schools: How to Harmonise Managing and Teaching for an Effective School.* London: Pearson Education.

Booth, T. and Ainscow, M. (2000) *Index for Inclusion: Developing Learning and Participation in Schools.* Bristol: Centre for Studies on Inclusive Education (CSIE).

British Educational Communications and Technology Agency (BECTA) (2000) *20 reasons why ICT is an excellent tool for teachers and learners.* Coventry: BECTA.

Corbett, J. (2001) *Supporting Inclusive Education: A connective pedagogy.* London: Routledge Falmer.

Department for Education and Employment (DfEE) (1997) *Excellence for all children: Meeting Special Educational Needs.* London: DfEE.

Department for Education and Employment (DfEE) (1998) *Meeting Special Educational Needs: A Programme of Action.* London: DfEE.

Department for Education and Employment (DfEE) (1999) *The National Curriculum: Handbook for Primary Teachers in England.* London: DfEE.

Department for Education and Employment (DfEE) (2000) *Transforming Secondary Education* – a pamphlet of a speech by David Blunkett to the Social Market Foundation. London: DfEE.

Department for Education and Employment (DfEE) and the National Association for Special Educational Needs (NASEN) (2001a) *Developing Support for More Inclusive Schooling: A review of the role of SEN Support Services in English LEAs.* Nottingham: DfEE.

Department for Education and Employment (DfEE) (2001b) *Advanced Skills Teachers: Promoting Excellence.* London: DfEE.

Department for Education and Employment (DfEE) (2001c) *Good Value CPD. A Code of Practice for Providers of Professional Development for Teachers.* London: DfEE.

Department for Education and Skills (DfES) (2001a) *Teachers' Standards Framework.* London: DfES.

Department for Education and Skills (DfES) (2001b) *Helping You Develop Guidance on Producing a Professional Development Record.* London: DfES.

Department for Education and Skills (DfES) (2001c) *Inclusive Schooling: Children with Special Educational Needs.* London: DfES.

Disability Equality in Education (1999) *Are You Prepared for the Future?* Publicity information leaflet. London: Disability Equality.

Dyson, A. and Gains, C. (1993) *Rethinking Special Needs in Mainstream Schools: Towards the Year 2000.* London: David Fulton Publishers.

European Foundation for Quality Management (EFQM) (2001) *Quality in Education: School self-assessment using the Excellence Model and improvement techniques.* London: Lloyds TSB.

Fleming, P. and Amesbury, M. (2001) *The Art of Middle Management in Primary Schools: A Guide to Effective Subject, Year and Team Leadership.* London: David Fulton Publishers.

Fletcher-Campbell, F. and Cullen, M.A. (1999) *Impact of Delegation on LEA Support Services for Special Educational Needs.* Berkshire: NFER.

Gains, C. and Smith, J. (1994) 'Cluster Models', *Support for Learning* 9(2), 94–98.

Hardy, C. (2000) *Information and Communications Technology for All.* London: David Fulton Publishers.

James, C. and Connolly, U. (2000) *Effective Change in Schools.* London: Routledge Falmer.

Lucas, B. and Greany, T. (2000) *Schools in the Learning Age.* London: Campaign for learning.

Lunt, I., Evans. J., Norwich, B. and Wedell, K. (1994) 'Collaborating to meet special educational needs: Effective Clusters', *Support for Learning* 9(2), 73–78.

Lunt, I. and Norwich, B. (1999) *Can effective schools be inclusive schools?* London: Institute of Education, University of London.

MacBeath, J. and Mortimore, P. (2001) *Improving School Effectiveness.* Buckingham: Open University Press.

MacBeath, J. and Myers, K. (1999) *Effective School Leaders. How to Evaluate and Improve Your Leadership Potential.* London: Pearson Education.

McKeown, S. (2000) *Unlocking Potential. How ICT can support children with special needs.* Birmingham: Questions Publishing.

National Association for Special Educational Needs (NASEN) (2000) *Policy Document on Professional Development.* Tamworth: NASEN.

National Association for Special Educational Needs (NASEN) (2001) *Policy Document on Learning Support Assistants.* Tamworth: NASEN.

National College for School Leadership (NCSL) (2001) *Springing Upward: New heights in leadership learning.* Nottingham: NCSL.

Nicholls, G. and Gardner, J. (1999) *Pupils in Transition Moving Between Key Stages.* London: Routledge.

O'Brien, T. (2001) *Enabling Inclusion: Blue Skies . . . Dark Clouds?* London: The Stationery Office.

Office for Standards in Education (OFSTED) (1999) *Handbook for Inspecting Primary Schools with guidance on self-evaluation.* London: OFSTED.

Office for Standards in Education (OFSTED) (2000) *Evaluating Educational Inclusion: Guidance for inspectors and schools.* London: OFSTED.

Office for Standards in Education (OFSTED) (2001a) *Advanced Skills Teachers: appointment, deployment and impact.* London: OFSTED.

Office for Standards in Education (OFSTED) (2001b) *Specialist Schools: An evaluation of progress.* London: OFSTED.

Office for Standards in Education (OFSTED) (2002a) *The Annual Report of Her Majesty's Chief Inspector of Schools: Standards and Quality in Education 2000/01.* London: OFSTED.

Office for Standards in Education (OFSTED) (2002b) *ICT in schools: Effect of government initiatives.* London: OFSTED.

Office for Standards in Education (OFSTED) (2002c) *Teaching Assistants in Primary Schools: An Evaluation of the Quality and Impact of their Work.* London: OFSTED.

Qualifications and Curriculum Authority (QCA) (1999) *Review of the National Curriculum for England.* Public consultation document. London: QCA.

Shaw, L. (2001) *Learning Supporters and Inclusion*. Bristol: CSIE.

Shropshire County Council/Telford and Wrekin Council (1999) *Mentoring*. Shrewsbury: Shropshire County Council.

Smith, D. (2000) *From Key Stage 2 to Key Stage 3: Smoothing the Transfer of Pupils with Learning Difficulties*. Tamworth: NASEN.

Teacher Training Agency (TTA) (1998) *National Standards for Subject Leaders*. London: TTA.

van Velzen, W., Miles, M., Eckholm, M., Hameyer, U. and Robin, D. (1985) *Making School Improvement Work*. Leuven: ACCO.

West, N. (1995) *Middle Management in the Primary School*. London: David Fulton Publishers.

Williams, S., Macalpine, A. and McCall, C. (2001) *Leading and Managing Staff Through Challenging Times*. London: The Stationery Office.

Woods, D. and Cribb, M. (2001) *Effective LEAs and School Improvement: Making a difference*. London: Routledge Falmer.

Index